best ever

 quick & easy

p

This is a Parragon Publishing Book
First published in 2003

Parragon Publishing
Queen Street House
4 Queen Street
Bath BA1 1HE
United Kingdom

Created and produced by
The Bridgewater Book Company Ltd,
Lewes, East Sussex

Photographer Ian Parsons
Home economists Sara Hesketh and Richard Green

ISBN: 1-40542-047-2

Printed in China

NOTE

This book uses imperial, metric, or US cup measurements. Follow the same units
of measurement throughout; do not mix imperial and metric. All spoon
measurements are level: teaspoons are assumed to be 5 ml and tablespoons
are assumed to be 15 ml. Unless otherwise stated, milk is assumed to be whole,
eggs and individual vegetables such as potatoes are medium, and pepper is
freshly ground black pepper.

The times given for each recipe are an approximate guide only because
the preparation times may differ according to the techniques used by
different people and the cooking times may vary as a result of the type of
oven used. Ovens should be preheated to the specified temperature. If using
a fan-assisted oven, check the manufacturer's instructions for adjusting the time
and temperature. The preparation times include chilling and marinating times,
where appropriate.

The nutritional information provided for each recipe is per serving or
per portion. Optional ingredients, variations or serving suggestions have
not been included in the calculations.

Recipes using raw or very lightly cooked eggs should be avoided
by infants, the elderly, pregnant women, convalescents, and anyone
suffering from an illness.

contents

introduction
4

soups & appetizers
14

salads & snacks
78

meat & poultry
120

fish & shellfish
170

desserts
210

index
254

introduction

Many people have hectic, busy lives these days with little time or desire to cook complicated meals every day. An increasing reliance on take-out foods, however convenient, can become expensive and unhealthy. This book demonstrates methods, tips and tricks for cooking fast, simple, tasty, and nutritious meals, mostly at little expense. Even if you do not generally enjoy cooking, you will find very easy recipes that even the worst cook will be pleased with at the end. Many of the recipes featured are lowfat and all are healthy and nutritious, essential for busy lifestyles that require lots of energy and vitality. When meals are cooked in just a few minutes, this leaves time to sit comfortably, relax and enjoy your food, reducing the risk of indigestion—a common problem for those who frequently eat "on the run." Step-by-step instructions and photographs of the key stages of preparation make the recipes easy to follow, ensuring that this book is a must for every busy person's kitchen.

Many of the recipes featured take less than 30 minutes from kitchen to table and some take even less time, allowing you to enjoy your creation, whether on your own or with a large group of friends and family. Each recipe includes an at-a-glance reference to the time it takes to prepare, although this will vary depending on your expertise, and the time it takes to cook. Most dishes can be served immediately, but a few benefit from being made in advance and chilled; this is flagged in the recipe.

Most homemade versions of salads, dressings, and sauces are far less expensive than the store-bought alternatives and are undoubtedly healthier, as you know exactly what ingredients have been added. Preparing food at home can give you a great sense of satisfaction, is much healthier for you and your family, and need not be time-consuming and messy. This book shows you an alternative way to ensure that preparing and cooking food is an enjoyable daily activity for you and your family, not a chore to dread or an inconvenience that you have to fit in round everything else.

fabulous fast food

There is a recipe here to suit every course, occasion, and family, whether you are single and need a speedy dinner before going out for the evening or have a very large family with disparate activities and hobbies and don't have time for a traditional Sunday roast. Asian dishes are traditionally quick to make and increasingly popular, so many favorites are featured here, such as Sesame Shrimp Toasts (see page 54) and Thai Golden Pouches (see page 61), which may be served as snacks or as impressive appetizers for guests. A recipe that can be adapted in countless ways, Singapore Noodles (see page 107), makes an ideal lunch or light evening meal for those on the run. Stir-fries are renowned for the speed in which they can be prepared and cooked, and Pork Stir-Fry (see page 132) is no exception. Chinese and other Asian dishes are also wonderful for entertaining, as you can easily prepare a smaller amount of several dishes and everybody is sure to find something to suit their particular tastes. Cooked using very little oil, they are particularly healthy for those watching their waistlines and cholesterol levels and are popular with people of all

& Figs (see page 74), and Mozzarella & Tomatoes (see page 75). These are ideal for entertaining at lunchtime, as is the French Salade Niçoise (see page 81), which can be prepared with canned or fresh tuna and is delicious served alfresco in the summer.

Many of the dishes recommended for entertaining look impressive, but are actually astonishingly easy to serve, simply by piling the various ingredients round and on top of each other in a decorative way. There are also more unusual and unfamiliar dishes that, at first glance, seem to require long and tedious preparation or special equipment, but which turn out to be far easier and quicker than you would think. Experiment with new flavors or rediscover classics—try Russian Salad (see page 88) or Chef's Salad (see page 86) in the summer or for a light meal, and Tournedos Rossini (see page 125), Chicken Teriyaki (see page 157), or Tarragon Chicken (see page 161) for a more filling dish. If you are a fan of fish and seafood, whether eating alone or throwing a dinner party, try Sole Meunière (see page 183), Veracruz Red Snapper (see page 186), or the Louisiana speciality Blackened Fish (see page 174). For something a little more exotic, try Thai Shrimp Curry (see page 202) or Balti Shrimp (see page 203).

Special desserts can also be quick and easy—you do not have to limit yourself to ice cream or fresh fruit. There are many desserts, both hot and cold, that are simple, healthy, and interesting. Refreshing and cooling Indian Mango Dessert (see page 222) is the ideal choice after a spicy curry or stir-fry and it is great as a summer snack as well. Many of these desserts, such as Zabaglione (see page 234) and Strawberry Baked Alaska (see page 241), look as if they have taken a lot of time and effort to

ages—from the very young and picky to the elderly. The range is vast: for example, Thai Fragrant Mussels (see page 209) is simplicity itself and well worth the cost for a special occasion, whereas Chinese Chicken (see page 158) is easy, yet economical and so appropriate for large families.

Many traditional Western dishes are also featured, such as Old English Cheese Soup (see page 26) and Mushroom Soup (see page 30) for a light lunch or appetizer and Chicken Cordon Bleu (see page 156) and Finnan Haddie (see page 177) for a satisfying main course. Recipes for those who have little time for shopping and find that they never have the right ingredients include Pantry Tuna (see page 111) and Toad in the Hole with Onion Gravy (see page 144). Some familiar dishes from round the world are the popular dips, Hummus (see page 68) and Guacamole (see page 69) from the Middle East and Mexico respectively, and the Italian Spaghetti alla Carbonara (see page 100), Prosciutto

prepare, yet are so simple that they almost seem like cheating. If you are fond of fruit and also have a sweet tooth, then you may want to try the Fruit Packages (see page 238), Lemon Posset (see page 242), Speedy Apricot Cheesecake (see page 246), or Fried Bananas in Maple Syrup (see page 248). These are just a few of the delicious desserts featured and you are sure to find one to complement the rest of the meal.

time-saving tips

There are many different ways to save time in the kitchen and you can use some or all of the methods together for really fast food. Quick and easy meals are very often highly nutritious, as the cooking methods preserve many of the important nutrients, particularly in vegetables.

Fast food techniques are nothing new—people have always been busy. In countries such as China, where historically fuel was scarce, this was an extra incentive to develop a way of cooking quickly, which resulted in the invention of the wok and stir-frying. Broiling, griddling, pan-frying, and stir-frying are the best techniques for cooking food quickly while preserving texture, color, and flavor. Some ingredients, such as chops and steaks, are best suited to broiling or griddling and others, such as chicken breast portions, can be cooked using whichever method suits you. Other options include poaching and baking in a package—moderately fast techniques that are especially suitable for cooking chicken, fish, and fruit. Use the recipes in this book as a guide to the best ways of cooking ingredients, as well as the best ways of presenting and serving them.

If you are used to a diet of slow-cooked casseroles or meat and two veg and you find that time is just not on your side, then you may have to re-educate yourself to produce fast and easy meals—for midweek family suppers anyway. Thinly sliced, diced, chopped, or grated ingredients cook significantly faster than chunky or whole

ones and also look attractive. Cooking vegetables this way makes them even healthier and preserves their texture.

Running a household, holding down a job, and feeding the family can be difficult to balance, so apply a little lateral thinking: you may find that one-pot meals are an ideal solution. They create less washing-up, make less mess in the kitchen in general, and often involve less chopping and peeling than many other dishes. If you are not fortunate enough to have a dishwasher, cleaning up at the end of a meal can often mean standing at the sink for long periods of time when you are full, tired, and need to get on with something else.

Often overlooked, one of the easiest ways to save time when cooking is not to in other words, to serve raw ingredients. As a main course or side dish, salads are the perfect choice—quick, easy, nutritious, and attractive. However, making the most of uncooked ingredients is not just limited to salads. You can serve raw vegetables, such as grated carrots, or canned mixed beans with cooked chicken or pasta dishes. Fresh bread and rolls are traditional accompaniments to meals throughout Europe, a pleasant habit worth adopting. Cheese requires little or no preparation and is ideal for adding flavor, color, texture, and substance to any meal. You can buy packages of ready-grated cheese at most supermarkets, although these are not so nice as freshly grated cheese. Parmesan and pecorino are ideal for adding a strong flavor to dishes and should be bought fresh in small quantities and grated as required.

Remember that you don't have to perform like a celebrity chef on television when you are in your own kitchen. Most of us cannot safely wield a chopping knife at that kind of speed and it isn't always necessary. Ingredients such as ham, bacon, chives, dill, sun-dried tomatoes, and anchovies can be chopped straight into the pan using a pair of kitchen scissors, saving time and cutting down on washing-up.

Pantry ingredients in jars and cans are invaluable for quick meals and you can make a satisfactory lunch or dinner using these alone. Consider canned ingredients, such as chopped tomatoes, baby corn, and sliced mushrooms, as rapid alternatives to fresh ingredients. Canned beans, such as mixed beans, kidney beans, lentils, and chickpeas, save an enormous amount of preparation time and are inexpensive. Olives, capers, and anchovies are great tossed into a salad to make it more interesting or can be coarsely chopped and added to many other dishes. Add capers sparingly, as they have a strong, pickled taste. Olives can be used as a garnish or as part of the dish; try both black olives and stuffed green olives, as they have very different flavors. Both go well with fish, including canned tuna and salmon. Canned fish can be the basis for a lunch or light dinner and needs only to be drained and flaked. Tuna, salmon, anchovy fillets, crabmeat, and sardines are valuable pantry stand-bys. You can base an entire meal round them or just add them to a vegetable dish for extra flavor, color, and protein. Sardines are rather oily, but the valuable omega-3 essential fatty acids are extremely good for you and the fish are tasty straight from the can, combined with a potato dish or salad. Most nuts will keep relatively well in a sealed container and can be used as a quick and easy garnish, but buy them in small quantities, as they will turn rancid if kept too long. Peanuts can also be used for a satay sauce or snack food, and pine nuts, walnuts, and cashews can all be added to food while cooking or sprinkled over before serving.

Ready-prepared vegetables are now widely available and are a great timesaver when you are entertaining, especially for recipes requiring carrots cut into thin sticks, cauliflower broken into small florets and similar fiddly foods. Many of these vegetables, which include carrots, baby corn, snow peas, cauliflower, and salads, can be eaten raw and will look attractive simply removed from their packaging and arranged on a serving plate. They are ideal for serving with dips at parties. Buying ready washed and trimmed vegetables is also a great timesaver and you may find these ingredients for almost the same price as unprepared varieties. The main disadvantage is that once vegetables have been cut, they start to lose their nutrients.

Many ready-made sauces can be used as instant flavoring for a variety of dishes and even those usually offered as condiments at the table can make interesting additions. Try mustard added to beef or chicken recipes and Worcestershire sauce added to soups and strongly flavored dishes. Many Asian sauces can be used for recipes other than those of Asian origin and there is a wide range available, including soy, hoisin, plum, black bean, and oyster sauce as well as Thai fish (also known as nam pla). Many of these Asian sauces are very strong and you need only a few drops. Light soy sauce has a saltier, weaker flavor and paler color than dark soy sauce—use it in a dish that requires no extra coloring. Dark soy sauce has a sweeter flavor and much darker color and adds an exotic touch to vegetable, rice, and noodle dishes as well as meat. No extra salt need be added to dishes with soy sauce in them. Tabasco sauce is made in Louisiana, the home of many spicy dishes. It can be added to soups, sauces, and braises to add moderate or fiery heat and is an easy alternative to chopping fresh chiles.

Dried mushrooms add an intense flavor to other ingredients, making the cost worthwhile. Using concentrated flavorings eliminates the need to reduce sauces—tomato paste, sun-dried tomatoes, bottled lemon juice, and bouillon cubes or bouillon powder add the flavor required without increasing the preparation or cooking time. For the best flavor, look for bouillon cubes that do not have too much added salt. Tomato paste is concentrated and you will need to add only a little to your cooking for a strong flavor and color. Sun-dried tomato paste is also readily available in most large supermarkets and makes wonderfully flavorsome sauces.

It has a darker color than standard tomato paste and a stronger, more distinctive flavor, so use sparingly. If you use tomato paste (sun-dried or normal) regularly, buy a jar, but as it can go moldy quickly, buying a small tube may be more economical. Store in the refrigerator.

Strained tomatoes are an Italian alternative to canned tomatoes. They are smoother than canned tomatoes and make a great base for sauces and soups and can be added to casseroles and stews with delicious results.

Pasta is an ideal foundation for many quick dishes, as it takes very little time to cook and requires no preparation. Fresh pasta can cook in as little as 2–3 minutes and most people find it tastier than dried varieties. However, dried pasta is a very useful pantry stand-by and is ready to serve within about 10 minutes. There are plenty of dried pasta varieties to choose from, such as tagliatelle, spaghetti, fusilli, penne, and farfalle, as well as ready-made sauces. These are useful if your time is quite limited and you want a very quick dish, which is tasty and nutritious. Many dishes traditionally served with potatoes, which take longer to cook, can be easily adapted to be served with pasta instead.

An Asian alternative to pasta, noodles are convenient, cook quickly and are healthy. They store well and will keep for a long time. Use noodles in soups and stir-fries and flavor with sesame oil and soy sauce. The easiest to buy and cook are egg noodles, which are inexpensive and come dried, usually in rectangular cakes. Rice noodles are also easy to cook and are available from many Asian supermarkets. As the name suggests, they are made from rice flour. Most noodles are of medium thickness, although you may find thicker ones in an Asian supermarket. Long, thin noodles are best used in soups and also in light sauces.

A fast and easy way to cook potatoes is in the microwave, this method being particularly suited to baked potatoes. In fact, most things, from meat to sauces, can be cooked in the microwave, although some foods are more suitable than others. Many foods will cook in round a quarter of the time they would take using conventional methods, and a microwave is very useful for thawing frozen complete dishes or individual ingredients. Although a microwave may save you time with many dishes, you may find you still have to stop and stir certain ingredients and foods, such as gravy and custard. Unlike a conventional oven, the more you put in the microwave, the longer it will take to cook, making it impractical for speedy meals. The microwave is a short-cut for softening butter, melting chocolate, and bringing citrus fruits to room temperature before squeezing.

forward planning

There is an old army saying that time spent in reconnaissance is never wasted and this is as true in the kitchen as it is on the front line. Being well organized and properly prepared in the kitchen is all the more important if you are short of time. Planning menus in advance avoids those occasions when you wander round the kitchen, poking about in the refrigerator, and rummaging in cupboards, wondering what to cook. Sit down at the weekend or before you go shopping with a pen and paper and plan the meals you are going to cook for the whole week. Don't begrudge the few minutes this will take you, as it will help you to feel more in control and more confident that you will succeed in getting meals ready in time and with the minimum of effort.

Shop selectively and plan properly. If you are planning a dish with a sauce, such as pesto, can you buy a palatable version of the sauce ready-made instead of making one yourself? Alternatively, if you use a particular sauce frequently, consider making a large batch in advance and storing it in convenient portions in the freezer. Jars of minced garlic are a time-saving alternative to fresh garlic and are usually very tasty. You can also buy gingerroot, cilantro, and some other herbs in jars; as long as you like the flavor, they save a lot of time and effort. However, bear in mind that it is sometimes not worth sacrificing flavor or texture for time. Are you really sure that powdered mashed potato is as nice as the real thing? Remember, too, to buy ingredients that you can use in more than one recipe, even in the same meal—sour cream can go with an appetizer and into a main course or crème fraîche can thicken a sauce for a main course and then be served with fruit for dessert. This saves a surprising amount of time that is often wasted finding ingredients, opening pots, adding and mixing, and also eliminates wastage.

Having a well-organized pantry and refrigerator are essential for making sure that you know where all the required ingredients are and to avoid having to stop to clean up spills caused by over-reaching for inaccessible items. It also helps avoid waste and disappointment, as you are less likely to overlook use-by dates on cans and packages or to leave something unidentified moldering into a new and furry life form in the salad drawer of the refrigerator.

Make sure that you have an adequate range of basic equipment, such as sharp knives, strainers, colanders, wooden spoons, and good-quality pans, as these will aid you in the speedy preparation of ingredients. Sharp knives are safer than blunt ones, too. Cutting boards are an essential item and will last a very long time. Invest in two, one for raw meat and seafood and the other for vegetables and cooked ingredients, as this will save your having to stop to clean a single board. Whether you prefer wood or plastic, select a good, solid board that will not slip easily.

Good-quality heavy-bottom pans are valuable investments, as they will ensure that the heat is evenly distributed through the pan, cooking your food faster and more evenly.

A wok is ideal for many quick dishes, not only those of Asian origin. The design ensures that the food is cooked evenly and it can be placed over very high heat, but it is important to buy a good-quality cast-iron wok, not a nonstick one, as the latter are not so reliable at very high temperatures. If you cook on an electric stove with a flat surface, select a wok with a flat bottom. A thick, solid bottom is very important to allow even distribution of heat. If the instructions tell you to season a wok before use, do so, as this improves the quality of cooking and the wok will last longer.

A ridged grill pan makes an attractive pattern on steaks and chops and can be used for many things, from kabobs to fish steaks. Buy cast-iron to ensure quality and make sure that you look after your kitchen equipment so that it lasts.

A solid, heavy-bottom, flameproof casserole can be costly, but is worth the money, as meals will be evenly cooked, moist, and flavorsome. You can use it on top of the stove to cook onions and sear meat at the start of a recipe and then to cook the rest of the dish, whether on the stove or in the oven, saving time and effort in both preparation and cleaning up afterward.

A steamer is a healthy way of cooking food and will not make vegetables, such as broccoli and cabbage, go soggy. It leaves them with a lovely texture and color and is useful for cooking more than one item at a time. You can set a steamer over a pan of water in which you have potatoes cooking and cook your broccoli and carrots in it, thereby cooking three things at once. Besides saving you time and energy, this is a more economical way of using fuel, too. As with any method of cooking, you can overcook in a steamer, but it is much harder to do so than by boiling for too long.

Measuring cups and spoons with clear, easy-to-read numbers are important. Although many dishes will not suffer from guesswork, some require exact measurements. Make sure you have imperial and metric measurements, but remember that they are not interchangeable.

There are many labor-saving kitchen tools on the market, most of which are inexpensive and readily available, but some tools are more useful than others. An electric can opener, for example, will save you a couple of seconds, while a food processor or electric whisk will save valuable minutes.

A solidly constructed, swivel-blade vegetable peeler is not only the easiest thing next to buying ready-peeled vegetables, but can be used for Parmesan and pecorino cheese shavings for an easy, attractive garnish.

Using a citrus zester is far easier than trying to grate lemon, lime, or orange rind and then scrape it from the inside of the grater.

Whatever equipment you are buying for the kitchen, from soup ladle to potato masher, choose good-quality brands with a reputable name, and care for and clean it properly to ensure that it will last you well. In addition, make sure that you have adequate storage space and that you have thought out where everything goes. Keep sharp knives, wooden spoons, and cutting boards near the counter or in drawers underneath it and store pans and woks near the stove. Save yourself lots of time and energy by planning your kitchen and keeping it clean and tidy: you do not want to be walking a marathon backward and forward across the kitchen in the middle of preparing dinner.

time-saving check list

- If you will need to use the oven or broiler, switch it on to preheat the moment you walk into the kitchen. Skimping on preheating doesn't save time and can risk food poisoning through inadequate cooking.

- Read the recipe before you start. You can save time by preparing some ingredients while others are cooking. Onions, for example, take at least 5 minutes to soften in a skillet of oil, so use this time to slice the meat, chop the carrots, or open a can of tomatoes.

- Fresh salad greens and delicate herbs, such as basil, bruise easily if sliced or chopped with a knife—it is both better and quicker to tear or shred them with your fingers.

- Using the appropriate size of pan for the ingredients makes cooking easier and quicker. There is no point heating up more liquid than you require or trying to stir an over-filled pan and constantly splashing the stove and possibly yourself.

- When cutting soft, creamy cheese, rinse the knife blade in cold water first to prevent sticking. This saves time and also prevents an uneven appearance.

- Mix Vinaigrette (see page 13) and other salad dressings in a screw-top jar by shaking them vigorously together. You can store any leftover dressing in the jar in the refrigerator for 2–3 days.

- Strip black currants and red currants from their stems by running the tines of a fork along the stem. Strip small leaves from herb sprigs by running the stem between your thumb and index finger.

- Foods cook more rapidly in metal or china containers than in earthenware or glass.

- If you prefer to make basic stocks, dressings, and vinaigrettes yourself, then the recipes on the opposite page can all be made in advance. The stocks can be stored in the freezer for 3–6 months and the vinaigrettes and dressings can be kept in screw-top jars in the refrigerator for 2–3 days. Shake or stir well before using.

basic recipes

vegetable stock

makes: about 2 quarts
preparation time: 10 minutes
cooking time: 35 minutes

2 tbsp corn oil
4 oz/115 g onions, finely chopped
4 oz/115 g leeks, finely chopped
4 oz/115 g carrots, finely chopped
4 celery stalks, finely chopped
3 oz/85 g fennel, finely chopped
3 oz/85 g tomatoes, finely chopped
9 cups water
1 bouquet garni

1 Heat the oil in a pan. Add the onions and leeks and cook over low heat for 5 minutes, or until softened. Add the remaining vegetables, cover, and cook for 10 minutes. Add the water and bouquet garni, bring to a boil, and let simmer for 20 minutes.

2 Strain, let cool, and store in the refrigerator. Use immediately or freeze in portions for up to 3 months.

chicken stock

makes: about 2½ quarts
preparation time: 15 minutes, plus 30 minutes chilling
cooking time: 3½ hours

3 lb/1.3 kg chicken wings and necks
2 onions, cut into wedges
4 quarts water
2 carrots, coarsely chopped
2 celery stalks, coarsely chopped
10 fresh parsley sprigs
4 fresh thyme sprigs
2 bay leaves
10 black peppercorns

1 Place the chicken wings and necks and the onions in a large, heavy-bottom pan and cook over low heat, stirring frequently, until lightly browned.

2 Add the water and stir to scrape off any sediment on the bottom of the pan. Bring to a boil, skimming off any

foam that rises to the surface. Add the remaining ingredients, partially cover, and let simmer gently for 3 hours.

3 Strain, let cool, and place in the refrigerator. When cold, discard the layer of fat on the surface. Use immediately or freeze in portions for up to 6 months.

beef stock

makes: about 7 cups
preparation time: 15 minutes, plus 30 minutes chilling
cooking time: 4½ hours

2 lb 4 oz/1 kg beef marrow bones, sawn into 3-inch/7.5-cm pieces
1 lb 7 oz/650 g stewing beef in 1 piece
3 quarts water
4 cloves
2 onions, halved
2 celery stalks, coarsely chopped
8 peppercorns
1 bouquet garni

1 Place the bones in the bottom of a large pan and place the stewing beef on top. Add the water and bring to a boil over low heat, skimming off any foam that rises to the surface.

2 Press a clove into each onion half and add to the pan with the celery, peppercorns, and bouquet garni. Partially cover, and simmer very gently for 3 hours. Remove the meat and simmer for 1 hour.

3 Strain, let cool, and place in the refrigerator. When cold, discard the layer of fat on the surface. Use immediately or freeze in portions for up to 6 months.

vinaigrette

makes: about 1 cup
preparation time: 5 minutes, plus 1 hour standing (optional)

⅔ cup extra virgin olive oil
5 tbsp white wine vinegar
or lemon juice

1 garlic clove, finely chopped
pinch of sugar
2 tsp Dijon mustard
1 tbsp chopped fresh parsley
salt and pepper

1 Place all the ingredients into a screw-top jar and shake vigorously.

2 If there is time, set the jar aside at room temperature for 1 hour to let the flavors infuse.

3 Shake well again before using. The vinaigrette may be stored in the jar in the refrigerator for 2–3 days. Shake well before using.

thousand island dressing

makes: about 1¾ cups
preparation time: 5 minutes

1¼ cups good-quality mayonnaise
5 tbsp mild chili sauce
2 tbsp tomato ketchup
2 scallions, finely chopped
1 hard-cooked egg, shelled and chopped
2 gherkins, finely chopped
1 tsp Dijon mustard

1 Place all the ingredients in a bowl and whisk well to mix.

2 Cover tightly with plastic wrap and let chill until required.

3 Stir the dressing again before serving chilled.

soups & appetizers

There is nothing quite so comforting and welcoming as homemade soup, but there is a common assumption that making it will somehow involve endless hours toiling over a bubbling pot in a steamy kitchen. Of course, some traditional soups do take a long time to cook and can involve lots of preparation, but there are others that are just as delicious and that can be made very quickly and easily. Within 20 minutes of getting home on a cold, dark night, you can serve a hungry family a satisfying tureen of Old English Cheese Soup (see page 26); in the same amount of time you can dish up a meal-in-a-bowl of Zuppa Pavese (see page 31) for a weekend lunch. With very little more effort, you can impress your dinner party guests with Spicy Crab Soup (see page 33).

This chapter also features other fabulously fast appetizers for entertaining and for family meals. Start dinner with a taste of the exotic with little "money bags" filled with a mixture of pork and crabmeat—Thai Golden Pouches (see page 61)—or ever-popular Sesame Shrimp Toasts (see page 54). A lavish platter of Antipasto Volente (see page 66) is the perfect choice for effortless entertaining and serving Scallops on Horseback (see page 46) with pre-dinner drinks will win hostess-of-the-year prizes. Set the mood for a long and lazy summer weekend lunch with Prosciutto & Figs (see page 74) or set the taste buds tingling with a sizzling plate of Vegetarian Fajitas (see page 71).

pumpkin soup

serves 4   **prep: 10 mins**   **cook: 35–40 mins**

This thick, creamy soup has a wonderful, warming golden color. It is flavored with fresh orange and thyme leaves.

INGREDIENTS

2 tbsp olive oil

2 medium onions, chopped

2 garlic cloves, chopped

2 lb/900 g pumpkin, peeled and cut into 1-inch/2.5-cm chunks

6 cups boiling Vegetable or Chicken Stock (see page 13)

finely grated rind and juice of 1 orange

3 tbsp fresh thyme leaves

salt and pepper

⅔ cup milk

crusty bread, to serve

NUTRITIONAL INFORMATION

Calories	111
Protein	. . . . .2g
Carbohydrate	. . . . .5g
Sugars	. . . . .4g
Fat	. . . . .6g
Saturates	. . . . .2g

variation

Try substituting a different fresh herb for the thyme, such as chopped tarragon, for a slightly different taste.

cook's tip

Pumpkins are usually large vegetables. To make things a little easier, ask the grocer to cut a chunk off for you. Alternatively, make double the quantity and freeze the soup for up to 3 months.

1 Heat the olive oil in a large pan. Add the onions to the pan and cook for 3–4 minutes, or until softened. Add the garlic and pumpkin and cook for an additional 2 minutes, stirring well.

2 Add the boiling Stock, orange rind and juice, and 2 tablespoons of the thyme to the pan. Let simmer, covered, for 20 minutes, or until the pumpkin is tender.

3 Place the mixture in a food processor and process until smooth. Alternatively, mash the mixture with a potato masher until smooth. Season to taste.

4 Return the soup to the pan and stir in the milk. Reheat for 3–4 minutes, or until piping hot, but not boiling. Sprinkle with the remaining fresh thyme just before serving out.

5 Ladle the soup into 4 warmed soup bowls and serve with crusty bread.

calabrian mushroom soup

serves 4 **prep: 5 mins** ⏲ **cook: 25–30 mins** ⏲

The Calabrian Mountains in southern Italy provide exotic mushrooms that give mushroom soup a rich flavor and color.

INGREDIENTS

2 tbsp olive oil

1 onion, chopped

1 lb/450 g mixed mushrooms, such as

cèpes, oyster, and white mushrooms

1¼ cups milk

3½ cups hot Vegetable Stock

(see page 13)

salt and pepper

8 slices of rustic bread or French stick

2 garlic cloves, crushed

1¾ oz/50 g butter, melted

scant ¾ cup Swiss cheese,

finely grated

NUTRITIONAL INFORMATION

Calories	.452
Protein	.15g
Carbohydrate	.42g
Sugars	.5g
Fat	.26g
Saturates	.12g

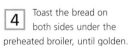

cook's tip

Mushrooms absorb liquid, which can lessen the flavor and affect cooking properties. Therefore, carefully wipe them with a damp cloth rather than rinsing them in water.

1 Preheat the broiler to medium. Heat the oil in a large skillet, add the onion and cook for 3–4 minutes, or until soft and golden.

2 Wipe each mushroom with a damp cloth and cut any large mushrooms into smaller, bite-size pieces. Add

the mushrooms to the skillet, stirring quickly to coat them in the oil.

3 Add the milk to the skillet, bring to a boil, cover, and let simmer for about 5 minutes. Gradually stir in the hot Vegetable Stock and season to taste with salt and pepper.

4 Toast the bread on both sides under the preheated broiler, until golden.

5 Mix the garlic and butter together. Spoon generously over the toast. Place the toast in the bottom of a large tureen or divide it between 4 individual serving bowls, then ladle over the

hot soup. Top with the grated Swiss cheese and serve at once.

tomato & pasta soup

cook: 50–55 mins   **prep: 5 mins**   **serves 4**

*Plum tomatoes are ideal for making soups and sauces
as they have denser, less watery flesh than rounder varieties.*

NUTRITIONAL INFORMATION

Calories 503

Protein 9g

Carbohydrate 59g

Sugars 16g

Fat 28g

Saturates 17g

INGREDIENTS

2 oz/55 g unsalted butter

1 large onion, chopped

2½ cups Vegetable Stock
(see page 13)

2 lb/900 g Italian plum tomatoes,
peeled and coarsely chopped

pinch of baking soda

8 oz/225 g dried fusilli

salt and pepper

1 tbsp superfine sugar

⅔ cup heavy cream

fresh basil leaves, to garnish

variation

To make orange and
tomato soup, simply use
half the quantity of
Vegetable Stock topped
up with the same amount
of fresh orange juice.

1 Melt the butter in a large pan, add the onion and cook for 3 minutes, stirring. Add half of the Stock to the pan with the chopped tomatoes and baking soda. Bring the soup to a boil, then reduce the heat and let simmer for 20 minutes. Remove from the heat and let cool.

2 Transfer the cooled soup to a food processor or blender and blend into a purée. Pour through a fine strainer back into the pan.

3 Add the remaining Vegetable Stock and the fusilli to the pan, and season to taste with salt and pepper. Add the sugar to the pan, bring to a boil, then reduce the heat and let simmer for 15 minutes.

 4 Ladle the soup into a warmed tureen, swirl the heavy cream over the surface and garnish with fresh basil leaves. Serve immediately.

vegetable & bean soup

serves 4   **prep: 30 mins**   **cook: 30 mins**

This filling soup is made from a wonderful combination of cannellini beans, fresh vegetables, and vermicelli, and is made even richer by the addition of pesto and dried porcini mushrooms.

INGREDIENTS

1 small eggplant	2 tsp dried basil
1 carrot	2 tbsp dried porcini mushrooms, soaked
1 leek	for 10 minutes in enough
2 large tomatoes	warm water to cover
1 potato, peeled	1¾ oz/50 g dried vermicelli
15 oz/425 g canned cannellini beans	3 tbsp store-bought pesto
3½ cups hot Vegetable or Chicken Stock	freshly grated Parmesan cheese,
(see page 13)	to serve (optional)

NUTRITIONAL INFORMATION

Calories 294

Protein 11g

Carbohydrate 30g

Sugars 2g

Fat 16g

Saturates 2g

variation

Bring a Mediterranean flavor to the soup by replacing the carrot, potato, and leek with chopped zucchini, red bell pepper, and cooked onion.

cook's tip

You can soften the eggplant slices before quartering them by placing them in a strainer and sprinkling them with salt. Set aside for 20 minutes to draw out the juices, then rinse in cold water.

1 Slice the eggplant into rings ½-inch/1-cm thick, then cut each ring into quarters. Cut the carrot into sticks 1-inch/2.5-cm long and cut the leek into rings. Cut the tomatoes and potato into small dice.

2 Place the cannellini beans and their liquid in a large pan. Add the eggplant, carrot, leek, tomatoes, and potatoes, stirring to mix. Add the Stock and bring to a boil, then let simmer for 15 minutes.

3 Add the basil, dried mushrooms and their soaking liquid, and the vermicelli and let simmer for 5 minutes, or until all of the vegetables are tender.

4 Remove the pan from the heat, stir in the pesto and serve immediately with freshly grated Parmesan cheese (if using).

artichoke soup

serves 4   **prep: 5 mins** ⏱   **cook: 15 mins** ⏱

This refreshing chilled soup is ideal for alfresco dining. Bear in mind that it needs to be chilled for 3–4 hours, so allow plenty of time.

INGREDIENTS

1 tbsp olive oil

1 onion, chopped

1 garlic clove, crushed

1 lb 12 oz/800 g canned artichoke hearts, drained

2½ cups hot Vegetable Stock (see page 13)

2 tbsp fresh thyme leaves

⅔ cup light cream

2 sun-dried tomatoes, cut into strips, to garnish

crusty bread, to serve (optional)

NUTRITIONAL INFORMATION

Calories	159
Protein	. . . . .2g
Carbohydrate	. . . . .5g
Sugars	. . . . .2g
Fat	. . . . .15g
Saturates	. . . . .6g

variation

Try adding 2 tablespoons of dry vermouth, such as Martini, to the soup in Step 5, if you wish.

1 Heat the oil in a large pan, add the onion and garlic, and cook, stirring constantly, for 2–3 minutes or until just softened.

2 Using a sharp knife, coarsely chop the artichoke hearts. Add them to the pan. Pour in the hot Vegetable Stock, stirring well. Bring the mixture to a boil,

then reduce the heat and let simmer, covered, for 3 minutes.

3 Transfer the soup to a food processor or blender and blend until smooth. Alternatively, push the mixture through a strainer to remove any lumps. Return the soup to the pan. Stir in the fresh thyme and light cream.

Transfer the soup to a large bowl and let cool, then cover and let chill in the refrigerator for about 3–4 hours.

4 Ladle the soup into 4 bowls and garnish with strips of sun-dried tomato. Serve with fresh crusty bread, if you like.

spinach & mascarpone soup

🕒 **cook: 35 mins**   🕐 **prep: 5 mins**   **serves 4**

Spinach is the basis for this delicious soup, but use sorrel or watercress instead for a pleasant change.

NUTRITIONAL INFORMATION

Calories 537

Protein 6g

Carbohydrate 9g

Sugars 2g

Fat . . . ., , ...53g

Saturates 29g

INGREDIENTS

2 oz/55 g butter

1 bunch scallions,
trimmed and chopped

2 celery stalks, chopped

generous 1 cup fresh spinach

3½ cups Vegetable Stock
(see page 13)

1 cup mascarpone cheese

salt and pepper

1 tbsp olive oil

2 slices thick-cut bread, cut into cubes

½ tsp caraway seeds

sesame breadsticks, to serve

variation

Any leafy vegetable can be made into a soup following this recipe. Try sorrel, watercress, young beet leaves, or lettuce instead of the spinach.

1 Melt half the butter in a large pan. Add the scallions and celery and cook gently for 5 minutes, or until softened.

2 Pack the spinach into the pan. Add the Vegetable Stock and bring to a boil, then reduce the heat and let simmer, covered, for 15–20 minutes.

3 Transfer the soup to a food processor or blender and blend until smooth. Alternatively, pass the mixture through a strainer. Return the soup to the pan. Add the mascarpone cheese and cook over low heat, stirring constantly, until smooth and blended. Season to taste with salt and pepper.

4 Heat the remaining butter with the oil in a skillet. Add the bread cubes and cook in the hot oil until golden brown. Add the caraway seeds toward the end of cooking, so that they do not burn.

5 Ladle the soup into 4 warmed bowls. Sprinkle the bread cubes

over the top and serve immediately, accompanied by the sesame breadsticks.

cream of pea soup

serves 4   **prep: 10 mins** ⏲   **cook: 18 mins** ⏲

This attractive, pale green soup is subtly flavored with mint and smoked salmon and would make a good first course for a dinner party. Serve with plenty of crusty bread, if you like.

INGREDIENTS

2 tbsp butter

1 onion, finely chopped

1 lb 5 oz/600 g frozen peas

3 cups Chicken Stock
(see page 13)

4 tbsp sour cream

4 oz/115 g smoked salmon, diced

2 tsp lemon juice

salt and pepper

2 fresh mint sprigs, leaves shredded

crusty bread, to serve

NUTRITIONAL INFORMATION

Calories 238

Protein 17g

Carbohydrate 18g

Sugars 6g

Fat 11g

Saturates 6g

variation

Use the same amount of fresh ready-shelled peas instead of frozen and substitute the mint with 1–2 teaspoons chopped fresh tarragon.

cook's tip

Using a hand-held electric blender to purée the soup in Step 2 will save both time and washing up. If you do not have time to make the Chicken Stock, use a good-quality bouillon cube instead.

1 Melt the butter in a large, heavy-bottom pan. Add the onion and cook over low heat, stirring occasionally, for 5 minutes, or until softened. Add the peas and Chicken Stock. Bring to a boil, cover, and let simmer gently for 10 minutes, or until the peas are tender.

2 Remove the pan from the heat and let cool slightly, then pour into a food processor and process until smooth. Alternatively, use a hand-held electric blender to purée the soup in the pan.

3 Return the soup to the pan, add the sour cream and return to a simmer. Stir in the smoked salmon and lemon juice and season to taste with salt and pepper. Sprinkle with the shredded mint, ladle into warmed soup bowls, and serve immediately with crusty bread.

old english cheese soup

serves 4   **prep: 10 mins**   **cook: 10 mins**

Ready in a matter of minutes, this is a filling and heart-warming soup. Serve with crusty bread as an antidote to winter's chills.

INGREDIENTS

2 oz/55 g butter

⅜ cup all-purpose flour

scant 2 cups Chicken Stock
(see page 13)

1¼ cups milk

2 carrots, grated

6 oz/175 g Cheddar cheese, grated

salt and pepper

crusty bread, to serve

NUTRITIONAL INFORMATION	
Calories	.390
Protein	.15g
Carbohydrate	.17g
Sugars	.6g
Fat	.30g
Saturates	.19g

variation

If you like, you can serve this soup with a few garlic croutons (see page 84, Step 2) sprinkled on top.

1 Melt the butter in a large, heavy-bottom pan. Sprinkle in the flour and cook, stirring constantly, for 1 minute. Remove the pan from the heat and gradually stir in the Chicken Stock and milk.

2 Return to the heat and bring to a boil, stirring constantly, then let simmer for 3–4 minutes, or until the soup is thickened and smooth. Add the grated carrots and let simmer for 3 minutes, then stir in the grated cheese.

3 When the cheese has melted, season to taste with salt and pepper. Ladle the soup into warmed soup bowls and serve immediately with crusty bread.

carrot & orange soup

⏱ **cook: 20 mins**   ⏲ **prep: 10 mins**   **serves 6**

Colorful and with a hint of sweetness, this classic soup can be served at any time of year.

NUTRITIONAL INFORMATION	
Calories	150
Protein	2g
Carbohydrate	19g
Sugars	13g
Fat	8g
Saturates	5g

INGREDIENTS

2 oz/55 g butter

2 onions, grated

salt and pepper

1 lb 9 oz/700 g carrots, grated

1 large potato, grated

2 tbsp grated orange rind

6–7 cups boiling water

juice of 1 large orange

2 tbsp chopped fresh parsley,
to garnish

cook's tip

To save time, squeeze the orange and chop the fresh parsley while the soup is simmering in Step 2 and use a hand-held electric blender to purée the soup.

1 Melt the butter in a large, heavy-bottom pan. Add the onions and cook over medium heat, stirring constantly, for 3 minutes. Sprinkle with a little salt, add the carrots and potato, then cover, reduce the heat, and cook for 5 minutes.

2 Stir the orange rind into the pan, then add enough boiling water to cover. Return to a boil, cover, and let simmer briskly for 10 minutes. Add the orange juice.

3 Remove the pan from the heat and let cool slightly, then pour into a food processor and process until a smooth purée forms. Alternatively, use a hand-held electric blender to purée the soup in the pan. Return the soup to the pan, adding a little more boiling water if it is too thick. Return to a boil, taste and adjust the seasoning if necessary, and ladle into warmed soup bowls. Garnish with chopped parsley and serve immediately.

tomato soup

serves 4   **prep: 10 mins** ⏲   **cook: 25 mins** ⏲

Soup made from fresh tomatoes is nothing like canned or packaged soups and is destined to become a firm family favorite.

INGREDIENTS

2 oz/55 g butter	2½ cups hot Chicken
1 onion, finely chopped	or Vegetable Stock (see page 13)
1 lb 9 oz/700 g tomatoes,	pinch of sugar
finely chopped	generous ⅓ cup light cream
salt and pepper	2 tbsp shredded fresh basil leaves
	1 tbsp chopped fresh parsley

NUTRITIONAL INFORMATION

Calories	.200
Protein	.3g
Carbohydrate	.11g
Sugars	.10g
Fat	.17g
Saturates	.11g

variation

Replace the chopped fresh parsley with the same amount of chopped fresh chives and serve with freshly grated Parmesan cheese sprinkled on the top.

cook's tip

If you like, peel the tomatoes while the onion is cooking in Step 1. Cut a cross in the base of each tomato, place in a bowl, and cover with boiling water. Leave for 1 minute, drain, and peel off the skins.

1 Melt half the butter in a large, heavy-bottom pan. Add the onion and cook over low heat, stirring occasionally, for 5 minutes, or until softened. Add the tomatoes, season to taste with salt and pepper, and cook for 5 minutes.

2 Pour in the hot Chicken Stock, return to a boil, then reduce the heat, and cook for 10 minutes.

3 Push the soup through a strainer with the back of a wooden spoon to remove the tomato skins and seeds. Return to the pan and stir in the sugar, cream, remaining butter, basil, and parsley. Heat through briefly, but do not let boil. Ladle into warmed soup bowls and serve immediately.

mushroom soup

serves 4   **prep: 10 mins** ⟁   **cook: 15–18 mins** ⟁

This is a tasty soup when made with ordinary cultivated mushrooms, but for a special occasion you could make it with exotic mushrooms for a more intense flavor.

INGREDIENTS

2 oz/55 g butter

1 onion, finely chopped

8 oz/225 g mushrooms, sliced

scant ¼ cup all-purpose flour

generous 2 cups hot Chicken Stock (see page 13)

⅔ cup milk

salt and pepper

1 tbsp chopped fresh parsley, plus extra to garnish

4 tbsp light cream

NUTRITIONAL INFORMATION

Calories	.200
Protein	.4g
Carbohydrate	.11g
Sugars	.5g
Fat	.16g
Saturates	.10g

variation

If you like a chunkier soup, do not process to a purée, simply season to taste with salt and pepper, and stir in the parsley and cream in Step 3.

1 Melt the butter in a large, heavy-bottom pan. Add the onion and cook over low heat, stirring occasionally, for 5 minutes, or until softened. Add the mushrooms and cook for 5 minutes.

2 Sprinkle in the flour and cook, stirring constantly, for 1 minute. Remove the pan from the heat and gradually stir in the hot Chicken Stock. Return to the heat and bring to a boil, stirring constantly. Stir in the milk.

3 Pour the soup into a food processor and process to a smooth purée, then return to the pan. Heat through briefly, season to taste with salt and pepper, and stir in the parsley and cream. Do not let the soup boil. Ladle into warmed soup bowls, garnish with chopped parsley, and serve immediately.

zuppa pavese

cook: 10 mins   **prep: 10 mins**   **serves 4**

It is important to use a good-quality, clear beef stock or consommé for this unusual Italian soup. It would make a lovely light lunch or first course for a dinner party.

NUTRITIONAL INFORMATION	
Calories	.320
Protein	.15g
Carbohydrate	.17g
Sugars	.1g
Fat	.22g
Saturates	.12g

INGREDIENTS

4 cups clear beef stock

or consommé

2 oz/55 g butter

4 slices white bread

½ cup freshly grated Parmesan cheese

4 eggs

salt

variation

Poach the eggs. Bring a pan of water to a boil, then simmer. Break an egg into a cup, stir the water, and slide in the egg. Cook for 3–4 minutes. Drain.

1 Pour the stock or consommé into a large, heavy-bottom pan and heat gently.

2 Meanwhile, melt the butter in a large, heavy-bottom skillet. Add the bread and cook over medium heat for 4–5 minutes, or until golden brown and crisp on both sides. Remove the cooked bread from the skillet, drain on paper towels, then place in the base of 4 large soup bowls.

3 Sprinkle two-thirds of the Parmesan cheese over the cooked bread. Break 1 egg on to each slice of cooked bread, season to taste with salt, and sprinkle with the remaining grated Parmesan cheese. Very carefully ladle the hot stock or consommé into the soup bowls and serve immediately.

spicy crab soup

cook: 15 mins   **prep: 10 mins**   **serves 4**

NUTRITIONAL INFORMATION	
Calories 95	
Protein 9g	
Carbohydrate 9g	
Sugars 2g	
Fat 0g	
Saturates 0g	

Use only white crabmeat for this Chinese-style soup, as the brown meat will disintegrate. You can use fresh, frozen, or canned crab.

INGREDIENTS

4 cups Chicken Stock	1 tbsp rice vinegar
(see page 13)	¾ tsp sugar
2 tomatoes, peeled and	1 tbsp cornstarch
finely chopped	2 tbsp water
1-inch/2.5-cm piece of fresh gingerroot,	6 oz/175 g white crabmeat, thawed
finely chopped	if frozen or drained if canned
1 small fresh red chile, seeded and	salt and pepper
finely chopped	2 scallions, shredded, to garnish
2 tbsp Chinese rice wine	

variation

If Chinese rice wine is not available, then use the same amount of dry sherry instead and replace the rice vinegar with white wine vinegar.

cook's tip

Chinese rice wine and rice vinegar are usually available from some large supermarkets as well as from specialist Asian food stores.

1 Pour the Chicken Stock into a large, heavy-bottom pan and add the tomatoes, ginger, chile, rice wine, vinegar, and sugar. Bring to a boil, then reduce the heat, cover, and let simmer for 10 minutes.

2 Mix the cornstarch and water together in a small bowl until a smooth paste forms, then stir into the soup. Let simmer, stirring constantly, for 2 minutes, or until slightly thickened.

3 Gently stir in the crabmeat and heat through for 2 minutes. Season to taste with salt and pepper, then ladle into warmed soup bowls and serve immediately, garnished with the shredded scallions.

lamb & rice soup

serves 4 **prep: 5 mins** **cook: 35 mins**

The addition of rice makes this a very filling and substantial soup, and the tender lamb and vegetables turn it into a full meal.

INGREDIENTS

5½ oz/150 g lean lamb

salt

scant ¼ cup rice

3½ cups lamb stock

1 leek, sliced

1 garlic clove, thinly sliced

2 tsp light soy sauce

1 tsp rice wine vinegar

1 medium open-cap mushroom, thinly sliced

NUTRITIONAL INFORMATION	
Calories 116	
Protein 9g	
Carbohydrate 12g	
Sugars 0.2g	
Fat 4g	
Saturates 2g	

variation

Use a few dried Chinese mushrooms, rehydrated as instructed on the package and chopped, instead of the open-cap mushroom. Add in Step 4.

1 Using a sharp knife, trim any visible fat from the lamb and cut the meat into thin strips. Set aside until required.

2 Bring a large pan of lightly salted water to a boil and add the rice. Return to a boil, stir once, reduce the heat, and cook for 10–15 minutes, or until tender.

Drain the cooked rice, rinse under cold running water, drain again, and set aside.

3 Place the lamb stock in a large pan and bring to a boil. Add the lamb strips, leek, garlic, soy sauce, and rice wine vinegar, reduce the heat, cover, and let simmer for 10 minutes, or until the lamb is tender and cooked through.

4 Add the mushroom slices and cooked rice to the pan and cook for an additional 2–3 minutes, or until the mushrooms are completely cooked through.

5 Ladle the soup into 4 warmed bowls and serve immediately.

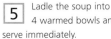

chunky potato & beef soup

⏲ **cook: 35 mins**   ◔ **prep: 5 mins**   **serves 4**

This is a real winter warmer—pieces of tender beef and chunky mixed vegetables are cooked in a liquor flavored with sherry.

NUTRITIONAL INFORMATION	
Calories 187	
Protein 14g	
Carbohydrate 12g	
Sugars 3g	
Fat 9g	
Saturates 2g	

INGREDIENTS

2 tbsp vegetable oil

8 oz/225 g lean braising steak, cut into strips

8 oz/225 g new potatoes, halved

1 carrot, diced

2 celery stalks, sliced

2 leeks, sliced

3½ cups Beef Stock (see page 13)

8 baby corn, sliced

1 bouquet garni

2 tbsp dry sherry

salt and pepper

chopped fresh parsley, to garnish

crusty bread, to serve

cook's tip

Make double the quantity of soup and freeze the remainder in a rigid container for later use. When ready to use, leave in the refrigerator to thaw thoroughly, then heat until piping hot.

1 Heat the vegetable oil in a large pan. Add the strips of meat to the pan and cook for 3 minutes, turning constantly. Add the potatoes, carrot, celery, and leeks to the pan. Cook for an additional 5 minutes, stirring.

2 Pour the Beef Stock into the pan and bring to a boil. Reduce the heat until the liquid is simmering, then add the baby corn and the bouquet garni. Cook for an additional 20 minutes, or until cooked through.

3 Remove and discard the bouquet garni. Stir the dry sherry into the soup, then season to taste with salt and pepper.

4 Ladle the soup into warmed bowls and garnish with chopped parsley. Serve with crusty bread.

mushroom & noodle soup

serves 4   **prep: 5 mins** ⏱   **cook: 10 mins** ⏱

A light, refreshing, clear soup of mushrooms, cucumber, and small pieces of rice noodles, flavored with soy sauce and a touch of garlic.

INGREDIENTS

4½ oz/125 g flat or
open-cap mushrooms
½ cucumber
2 scallions
1 garlic clove

2 tbsp vegetable oil
2½ cups water
1 oz/25 g Chinese rice noodles
¾ tsp salt
1 tbsp soy sauce

NUTRITIONAL INFORMATION

Calories 84

Protein 1g

Carbohydrate 3g

Sugars 1g

Fat 8g

Saturates 1g

variation

For a little extra spice, add a chopped fresh red chile to the soup with the scallions and garlic in Step 2.

cook's tip

Scooping the seeds out from the cucumber gives it a prettier effect when sliced, and also helps to reduce any bitterness, but if you prefer, you can leave them in.

1 Wash the mushrooms and pat dry with paper towels. Slice thinly. Do not remove the peel, as this adds more flavor. Halve the cucumber lengthwise. Scoop out the seeds using a teaspoon, then slice the flesh thinly. Chop the scallions finely and cut the garlic clove into thin strips.

2 Heat the oil in a large preheated wok or pan. Add the scallions and garlic and stir-fry for 30 seconds. Add the mushrooms and stir-fry for 2–3 minutes.

3 Stir in the water. Break the noodles into short lengths and add to the soup. Bring to a boil, stirring.

4 Add the cucumber slices, salt, and soy sauce, and let simmer for 2–3 minutes.

5 Ladle the soup into warmed bowls, distributing the noodles and vegetables evenly.

chicken & leek soup

serves 4–6   **prep: 5 mins** (L   **cook: 1 hr 15 mins**

This fresh, satisfying soup, packed full of protein and fiber, is substantial enough to be served as a main course. If you like, you can add a touch of color with some diced red bell pepper.

INGREDIENTS

2 tbsp butter
12 oz/350 g boneless chicken
12 oz/350 g leeks, cut into
1-inch/2.5-cm pieces
5 cups Chicken Stock
(see page 13)
1 bouquet garni envelope
salt and white pepper
8 pitted prunes, halved
scant 1 cup cooked rice
1 red bell pepper, diced (optional)

NUTRITIONAL INFORMATION

Calories	.183
Protein	.21g
Carbohydrate	.4g
Sugars	.4g
Fat	.9g
Saturates	.5g

 **1** Melt the butter in a large pan. Add the chicken and leeks and cook for 8 minutes.

2 Add the Chicken Stock and bouquet garni envelope to the pan and stir well, then season to taste

with salt and pepper. Bring to a boil and let simmer for 45 minutes.

3 Add the prunes to the pan with the cooked rice and diced bell pepper (if using) and let simmer for 20 minutes.

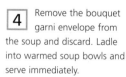

4 Remove the bouquet garni envelope from the soup and discard. Ladle into warmed soup bowls and serve immediately.

variation

Instead of the bouquet garni envelope, you can use a bunch of fresh mixed herbs, tied together with string. Choose herbs such as parsley, thyme, and rosemary.

partan bree

⏱ **cook: 35 mins**   ⏲ **prep: 1 hr**   **serves 6**

This traditional Scottish soup is based on fish stock, thickened with a delicious purée of rice and crabmeat cooked in milk, and flavored with citrus juice and anchovy extract.

NUTRITIONAL INFORMATION

Calories	112
Protein	7g
Carbohydrate	18g
Sugars	5g
Fat	2g
Saturates	0.3g

INGREDIENTS

1 medium-size boiled crab

generous ⅜ cup long-grain rice

2½ cups skim milk

salt and pepper

2½ cups fish stock

1 tbsp anchovy extract

2 tsp lime or lemon juice

1 tbsp chopped fresh parsley or l tsp chopped fresh thyme

3–4 tbsp sour cream (optional)

snipped fresh chives, to garnish

cook's tip

If you are unable to buy a whole crab, use 6 oz/175 g frozen crabmeat and thaw thoroughly before use, or 6 oz/175 g canned crabmeat, thoroughly drained.

1 Remove and set aside all the brown and white meat from the body of the crab. Crack the claws, remove and chop the meat, and set aside.

2 Place the rice and milk in a pan and bring slowly to a boil. Cover and let simmer gently for 20 minutes.

3 Add the reserved brown and white meat from the body of the crab, season to taste with salt and pepper and let simmer for an additional 5 minutes. Let the mixture cool slightly, then transfer to a food processor or blender and blend until smooth. Alternatively, press the mixture through a strainer.

4 Pour the soup into a clean pan and add the fish stock and reserved claw meat. Bring slowly to a boil, then add the anchovy extract and lime juice and adjust the seasoning. Let simmer for an additional 2–3 minutes.

5 Stir in the herbs, then ladle into warmed soup bowls. Swirl a little sour cream through each serving (if using). Garnish with snipped fresh chives and serve.

spicy dal & carrot soup

serves 6   **prep: 10 mins**   **cook: 50 mins**

This warming and nutritious soup includes a selection of spices to give it a "kick." It is simple to make and extremely good to eat.

INGREDIENTS

generous ⅝ cup split red lentils	1 tsp ground coriander
5 cups Vegetable Stock	1 fresh green chile, seeded
(see page 13)	and chopped
12 oz/350 g carrots, sliced	½ tsp ground turmeric
2 onions, chopped	1 tbsp lemon juice
9 oz/250 g canned chopped tomatoes	salt
2 garlic cloves, chopped	1¼ cups skim milk
2 tbsp vegetable ghee or oil	2 tbsp chopped fresh cilantro
1 tsp ground cumin	plain yogurt, to serve

NUTRITIONAL INFORMATION

Calories	173
Protein	9g
Carbohydrate	24g
Sugars	11g
Fat	5g
Saturates	1g

variation

If you can't find a fresh green chile, you can substitute 1 teaspoon of minced chile from a jar.

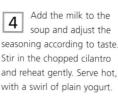

cook's tip

Make double the quantity of soup and freeze the remainder in a rigid container for later use. When ready to use, leave in the refrigerator to thaw thoroughly, then heat until piping hot.

1 Place the lentils in a strainer and wash well under cold running water. Drain and place in a large pan with 3½ cups of the Vegetable Stock, the carrots, onions, tomatoes, and garlic. Bring the mixture to a boil, then reduce the heat, cover, and let simmer for 30 minutes.

2 Meanwhile, heat the ghee in a small pan, add the cumin, coriander, chile, and turmeric and cook gently for 1 minute. Remove from the heat and stir in the lemon juice and salt to taste.

3 Purée the soup in batches in a food processor or blender. Return the soup to the pan, add the spice mixture and the remaining Stock and let simmer for 10 minutes.

4 Add the milk to the soup and adjust the seasoning according to taste. Stir in the chopped cilantro and reheat gently. Serve hot, with a swirl of plain yogurt.

red lentil soup with yogurt

serves 4   **prep: 5 mins** ⏲   **cook: 30 mins** ⏱

This tasty red lentil soup, made in the microwave, is delicately flavored with chopped cilantro. The yogurt adds a light piquancy.

INGREDIENTS

2 tbsp butter

1 onion, chopped finely

1 celery stalk, chopped finely

1 large carrot, grated

1 dried bay leaf

generous 1 cup split red lentils

5 cups hot Vegetable or Chicken Stock (see page 13)

salt and pepper

2 tbsp chopped fresh cilantro

4 tbsp low fat plain yogurt

fresh cilantro sprigs, to garnish

NUTRITIONAL INFORMATION

Calories	.280
Protein	.17g
Carbohydrate	.40g
Sugars	.6g
Fat	.7g
Saturates	.4g

cook's tip

For an extra creamy soup try adding the same amount of low fat sour cream instead of the plain yogurt in Step 4.

1 Place the butter, onion, and celery in a large bowl. Cover and cook on High power for 3 minutes.

2 Add the carrot, bay leaf, and lentils. Pour over the Stock. Cover and cook on High power for 15 minutes, stirring halfway through. Remove from the microwave, cover, and let stand for 5 minutes. Remove the bay leaf, then transfer in batches to a food processor or blender and blend until smooth. Alternatively, push the mixture through a strainer.

3 Pour into a clean bowl. Season to taste and stir in the cilantro. Cover and cook on High power for 4–5 minutes, until piping hot.

4 Ladle into warmed bowls. Stir 1 tablespoon of yogurt into each serving and garnish with sprigs of fresh cilantro.

yogurt & spinach soup

⏱ **cook: 30 mins**   ◔ **prep: 15 mins**   **serves 4**

Whole young spinach leaves add vibrant color to this unusual soup.
Serve with hot, crusty bread for a nutritious light meal.

NUTRITIONAL INFORMATION	
Calories	227
Protein	14g
Carbohydrate	29g
Sugars	13g
Fat	7g
Saturates	2g

INGREDIENTS

2½ cups Chicken Stock
(see page 13)
salt and pepper
scant ⅓ cup long-grain rice,
rinsed and drained
4 tbsp water
1 tbsp cornstarch
2½ cups low fat plain yogurt
3 egg yolks, lightly beaten
juice of 1 lemon
generous 1 cup fresh young spinach
leaves, washed and drained
crusty bread, to serve

variation

You can substitute watercress for the spinach If you prefer, but cut off any tough stalks and use only the tender leaves.

1 Pour the Stock into a pan, season to taste with salt and pepper, and bring to a boil. Add the rice and let simmer for 10 minutes, until barely cooked. Remove from the heat.

2 Combine the water and cornstarch to make a smooth paste.

3 Pour the yogurt into a separate pan and stir in the cornstarch paste. Set over low heat and bring slowly to a boil, stirring with a wooden spoon in one direction only. This prevents the yogurt curdling on contact with the hot stock. When it has reached boiling point, stand the pan on a heat diffuser and let simmer gently for 10 minutes. Remove the pan from the heat and let cool slightly, then stir in the egg yolks.

4 Pour the yogurt mixture into the stock, add the lemon juice and stir to blend thoroughly. Keep warm, but do not let boil.

5 Blanch the spinach in a pan of lightly salted boiling water for 2–3 minutes, until softened, but not wilted. Drain well, then stir into the soup. Let the spinach warm through. Taste the soup and adjust the seasoning, if necessary. Serve in wide, shallow soup plates, with hot, fresh crusty bread.

thick onion soup

serves 6 **prep: 20 mins** **cook: 1 hr 10 mins**

This delicious, creamy soup is made with grated carrot and parsley to give extra texture and color. Serve with crusty cheese biscuits to turn it into a hearty lunch.

INGREDIENTS

2¾ oz/75 g butter

1 lb 2 oz/500 g onions, finely chopped

1 garlic clove, crushed

generous ¼ cup all-purpose flour

2½ cups Vegetable Stock (see page 13)

2½ cups milk

salt and pepper

2 tsp lemon or lime juice

good pinch of ground allspice

1 bay leaf

1 carrot, coarsely grated

4–6 tbsp heavy cream

2 tbsp chopped fresh parsley, to garnish

CHEESE BISCUITS

1¾ cups malted wheat or whole-wheat flour

2 tsp baking powder

2 oz/55 g butter

4 tbsp freshly grated Parmesan cheese

1 egg, beaten

about ¼ cup milk

NUTRITIONAL INFORMATION

Calories 277

Protein 6g

Carbohydrate 19g

Sugars 12g

Fat 20g

Saturates 8g

variation

Knead 1 tablespoon of finely snipped fresh chives into the cheese biscuit dough at the end of Step 2.

cook's tip

Keep a little extra lemon or lime juice to hand in case you want to add more flavor to the soup before serving. Stir it in just before adding the cream in Step 4.

1 Melt the butter in a pan, add the onions and garlic, and cook over low heat, stirring frequently, for 10–15 minutes, until softened, but not colored. Add the flour and cook, stirring, for 1 minute, then gradually stir in the Stock and bring to a boil, stirring frequently. Add the milk, then return the mixture to a boil. Season to taste with salt and

pepper and add the lemon juice, allspice, and bay leaf. Cover and let simmer for 25 minutes, or until the vegetables are tender. Remove and discard the bay leaf.

2 Meanwhile, make the biscuits. Preheat the oven to 425°F/220°C. Combine the flour, baking powder, and seasoning and rub in the

butter until the mixture resembles fine bread crumbs. Stir in 3 tablespoons of the cheese, the egg, and enough milk to mix to a soft dough.

3 Shape the dough into a bar about ¾-inch/2-cm thick. Place on a floured cookie sheet and mark into slices. Sprinkle with the remaining cheese and bake in the oven

for 20 minutes, or until risen and golden brown.

4 Stir the carrot into the soup and let simmer for 2–3 minutes. Add more lemon juice, if necessary. Stir in the cream and reheat. Garnish with chopped parsley and serve with the warm biscuits.

scallops on horseback

serves 4　　　　　　**prep: 5 mins** ⏲　　　　　　**cook: 10 mins** ⏲

These tasty little morsels would make wonderful hot canapés to serve with pre-dinner drinks.

INGREDIENTS

20 prepared scallops, thawed if frozen

2–3 tbsp lemon juice

salt and pepper

20 rindless lean bacon slices

tartare sauce, to serve

NUTRITIONAL INFORMATION	
Calories 485	
Protein 53g	
Carbohydrate 4g	
Sugars 0g	
Fat 29g	
Saturates 10g	

1 Preheat the broiler to medium. Sprinkle the scallops with lemon juice and season to taste with salt and pepper.

2 Stretch the bacon with a flat-bladed knife, then wrap a slice round each scallop, securing it with a wooden toothpick.

3 Cook under the preheated broiler for 5 minutes on each side, or until cooked through. Serve immediately with tartare sauce.

cook's tip

For a speedy tartare sauce, stir 2 tablespoons each chopped gherkins and capers into 1¼ cups ready-made mayonnaise. Stir in chopped chives or finely chopped scallions to taste and serve.

pan-fried scallops & shrimp

⏱ **cook: 4 mins**   ⏱ **prep: 10 mins**   **serves 4**

As most shellfish needs very little cooking, it is the perfect choice for the cook in a hurry. It also looks attractive and tastes wonderful.

NUTRITIONAL INFORMATION	
Calories 225	
Protein 24g	
Carbohydrate 11g	
Sugars 0g	
Fat 10g	
Saturates 2g	

INGREDIENTS

12 prepared scallops, thawed if frozen

12 large raw shrimp, shelled
and deveined

salt and pepper

2 tbsp all-purpose flour

3 tbsp olive oil

2 garlic cloves, finely chopped

2 tbsp chopped fresh parsley

3 tbsp lemon juice

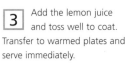

cook's tip

If using frozen scallops, thaw out slowly in the refrigerator. Once they are completely thawed out, use immediately, or keep in the refrigerator until ready to cook, but use on the same day.

1 Using a sharp knife, cut the scallops in half, then season the scallops and shrimp with salt and pepper to taste. Spread the flour out on a plate and use to dust the scallops and shrimp, shaking off the excess.

2 Heat the olive oil in a large, heavy-bottom skillet. Add the floured scallops and shrimp and cook over medium heat for 2 minutes. Add the chopped garlic and parsley, then stir well, tossing the shellfish to coat, and cook, shaking the skillet occasionally,

for 2 minutes, or until the scallops are opaque and the shrimp have changed color.

3 Add the lemon juice and toss well to coat. Transfer to warmed plates and serve immediately.

bell pepper salad

serves 4   **prep: 5–10 mins** ⟳   **cook: 35 mins** ⏱

Colorful marinated Mediterranean vegetables make a tasty appetizer, especially when served with fresh bread or Tomato Toasts.

INGREDIENTS

1 onion	TOMATO TOASTS
2 red bell peppers	small stick of French bread
2 yellow bell peppers	1 garlic clove, crushed
3 tbsp olive oil	1 tomato, peeled and chopped
2 large zucchinis, sliced	2 tbsp olive oil
2 garlic cloves, sliced	salt and pepper
1 tbsp balsamic vinegar	
1¾ oz/50 g anchovy fillets, chopped	
2 tbsp black olives,	
halved and pitted	
salt and pepper	
1 tbsp chopped fresh basil	

variation

If you like, chop an eggplant into chunks, sprinkle with salt to draw out the juices, then rinse and add in Step 2 with an extra tablespoonful of oil.

cook's tip

If you find canned anchovies rather too salty, soak them in a saucer of cold milk for 5 minutes, then drain and pat dry with paper towels before using. The milk absorbs the salt.

1 Cut the onion into wedges. Core and seed the bell peppers and cut into thick slices.

2 Heat the oil in a heavy-bottom skillet. Add the onion, bell peppers, zucchinis, and garlic and cook gently for 20 minutes, stirring occasionally.

3 Add the vinegar, anchovies, olives, and seasoning to taste, mix thoroughly and let cool. Spoon the cooled mixture onto individual plates and sprinkle with the basil.

4 To make the Tomato Toasts, preheat the oven to 425°F/220°C. Cut the French bread diagonally into ½-inch/1-cm slices. Mix the garlic, tomato, oil, and seasoning together, and spread thinly over each slice of bread.

5 Place the bread on a cookie sheet and bake in the preheated oven for 5–10 minutes, until crisp. Serve with the vegetable salad.

flambéed shrimp

serves 4   **prep: 10 mins**   **cook: 20 mins**

Serve these fabulous hot shrimp with a small portion of colorful salad greens, such as oak leaf lettuce, radicchio, or lollo rosso.

INGREDIENTS

3 tbsp butter

2 shallots, chopped

8 oz/225 g cooked shelled shrimp

4 oz/115 g white mushrooms, halved

1 tbsp lemon juice

pinch of freshly grated nutmeg

salt and pepper

3 tbsp brandy

⅔ cup heavy cream

fresh flatleaf parsley sprigs, to garnish

mixed salad greens, to serve

NUTRITIONAL INFORMATION

Calories	.335
Protein	.14g
Carbohydrate	.2g
Sugars	.2g
Fat	.27g
Saturates	.17g

variation

You could use raw shrimp rather than cooked. Add them in Step 1 with the mushrooms and cook for 5 minutes, or until they have changed color.

1 Melt the butter in a large, heavy-bottom skillet. Add the shallots and cook over low heat, stirring occasionally, for 5 minutes. Add the shrimp and mushrooms and cook, stirring occasionally, for 3–4 minutes, then season to taste with lemon juice, nutmeg, salt, and pepper.

2 Measure the brandy into a metal ladle and warm over very low heat. Ignite and pour the flaming brandy over the shrimp mixture. Shake the skillet gently until the flames have died down, then cook for an additional 2–3 minutes.

3 Stir in the cream, increase the heat, and cook, stirring constantly, until thickened. Divide between warmed serving plates, garnish with the parsley sprigs, and serve immediately with mixed salad greens.

tagliarini with gorgonzola

⏲ **cook: 20 mins**   ⏱ **prep: 5 mins**   **serves 4**

This simple, creamy pasta sauce is a classic Italian recipe. You could use Danish blue cheese instead of the Gorgonzola, if you prefer.

NUTRITIONAL INFORMATION	
Calories	904
Protein	. . . . .27g
Carbohydrate	. . . . .83g
Sugars	. . . . .4g
Fat	. . . . .53g
Saturates	. . . . .36g

INGREDIENTS

2 tbsp butter

8 oz/225 g Gorgonzola cheese, coarsely crumbled

⅔ cup heavy cream

2 tbsp dry white wine

1 tsp cornstarch

4 fresh sage sprigs, finely chopped

salt and white pepper

14 oz/400 g dried tagliarini

2 tbsp olive oil

cook's tip

When buying Gorgonzola, always check that it is creamy yellow with delicate green veining. Avoid hard or discolored cheese. It should have a rich, piquant aroma, not a bitter smell.

1 Melt the butter in a heavy-bottom pan. Stir in 6 oz/175 g of the cheese and melt, over low heat, for 2 minutes.

2 Add the cream, white wine, and cornstarch and beat with a whisk until fully incorporated.

3 Stir in the sage and season to taste with salt and white pepper. Bring to a boil over low heat, whisking constantly, until the sauce thickens. Remove from the heat and set aside while you cook the pasta.

4 Bring a large pan of lightly salted water to a boil. Add the tagliarini and 1 tablespoon of the olive oil. Cook the pasta for 8–10 minutes, or until just tender, then drain thoroughly and toss in the remaining olive oil. Transfer the pasta to a serving dish and keep warm.

5 Reheat the Gorgonzola sauce over low heat, whisking constantly. Spoon the sauce over the tagliarini, generously sprinkle over the remaining cheese, and serve.

smoked trout with pears

 cook: 0 mins   prep: 10 mins   serves 4

NUTRITIONAL INFORMATION

Calories 329

Protein 37g

Carbohydrate 11g

Sugars 10g

Fat 16g

Saturates 4g

Trout is hot-smoked, so needs no further cooking—a boon when you are short of time. The fillets should be a delicate beige-pink color. Avoid darker ones, which will have been artificially colored.

INGREDIENTS

1¼ cups watercress or arugula

1 head of radicchio, torn into pieces

4 smoked trout fillets, skinned

2 ripe pears, such as Bartlett

2 tbsp lemon juice

2 tbsp extra virgin olive oil

salt and pepper

3 tbsp sour cream

2 tsp creamed horseradish

thinly sliced brown bread, crusts removed and buttered, to serve

variation

Replace the horseradish with mustard mayonnaise. Mix 3 teaspoons mustard, 2 teaspoons chopped fresh dill, and ⅔ cup mayonnaise. Season.

cook's tip

Olive oil is very versatile as it can be used for sautéing, cooking, and salad dressings. Use the best-quality extra virgin olive oil that you can find in dressings and use the ordinary virgin olive oil in cooking.

1 Place the watercress and radicchio in a bowl. Cut the trout fillets into thin strips and add to the bowl. Halve and core the pears, then slice thinly. Place in a separate bowl, add 4 teaspoons of the lemon juice, and toss to coat. Add the pears to the salad.

2 To make the dressing, mix the remaining lemon juice and the olive oil together in a bowl, then season to taste with salt and pepper. Pour the dressing over the salad and toss well. Transfer to a large salad bowl.

3 Mix the sour cream and horseradish together in a separate bowl until thoroughly blended, then spoon over the salad. Serve with buttered brown bread.

sesame shrimp toasts

serves 4　　　　　**prep: 10 mins** ⟲　　　　　**cook: 4–6 mins** ♨

One of the most popular Chinese appetizers, these crisp, golden and succulent little toasts take only a few minutes to prepare.

INGREDIENTS

8 oz/225 g raw shrimp, shelled and deveined

2 tbsp shortening

1 egg white, lightly beaten

1 tsp chopped scallions

½ tsp finely chopped fresh gingerroot

1 tbsp Chinese rice wine or dry sherry

1 tsp cornstarch

2 tsp water

salt and pepper

6 slices white bread, crusts removed

⅝ cup sesame seeds

peanut oil, for deep-frying

NUTRITIONAL INFORMATION	
Calories	.445
Protein	.15g
Carbohydrate	.23g
Sugars	.1g
Fat	.33g
Saturates	.7g

variation

If you cannot find peanut oil for deep-frying, then use vegetable or corn oil instead.

cook's tip

If you are using a wok, preheat it first without any oil until hot. This prevents the food sticking and ensures an even distribution of heat while cooking.

1 Place the shrimp and shortening on a cutting board and chop them together until they form a paste. Scrape into a bowl and stir in the egg white, scallions, ginger, and rice wine. Mix the cornstarch and water together in a small bowl until a smooth paste forms, then stir into the shrimp mixture and season to taste with salt and pepper.

2 Spread the shrimp paste evenly over one side of each slice of bread. Spread out the sesame seeds on a flat plate or sheet and gently press the spread side of each slice of bread into the seeds to coat.

3 Heat the peanut oil in a preheated wok or large skillet. Add half the slices of bread, spread-side down, and cook for 2–3 minutes, or until golden brown. Remove with a slotted spoon and drain on paper towels. Cook the remaining slices in the same way. Cut each slice into fingers and serve immediately.

chinese omelet

serves 4　　　　**prep: 5 mins** ⏲　　　　**cook: 5 mins** ⏲

This is a fairly filling omelet, as it contains chicken and shrimp.
It is cooked as a whole omelet, then sliced for serving.

INGREDIENTS

8 eggs

8 oz/225 g cooked chicken, shredded

12 raw jumbo shrimp, shelled
and deveined

2 tbsp snipped fresh chives

2 tsp light soy sauce

dash of chili sauce

2 tbsp vegetable oil

NUTRITIONAL INFORMATION

Calories	.309
Protein	.34g
Carbohydrate	.0.2g
Sugars	.0g
Fat	.19g
Saturates	.5g

1 Lightly beat the eggs in a large mixing bowl. Add the shredded chicken and jumbo shrimp to the eggs and mix well.

2 Stir in the snipped chives, soy sauce, and chili sauce, mixing well to combine all the ingredients.

3 Preheat a large skillet over medium heat. Add the vegetable oil. When the oil is hot, add the egg mixture to the skillet, tilting the skillet to coat the bottom completely. Cook over medium heat, gently stirring the omelet with a fork, until the surface is just set and the underside is golden brown.

4 When the omelet is set, slide it out of the skillet using a spatula.

5 Cut the Chinese omelet into squares or slices and serve. Alternatively, serve the omelet as a main course for two people.

variation

Add extra flavor by stirring in 3 tablespoons of finely chopped fresh cilantro or 1 teaspoon of sesame seeds with the chives in Step 2.

crispy seaweed

⏱ **cook: 5 mins**   ⏲ **prep: 10 mins**   **serves 4**

This tasty Chinese appetizer is not all that it seems—the "seaweed" is in fact bok choy, which is cooked, salted, and tossed with pine nuts.

NUTRITIONAL INFORMATION	
Calories	.214
Protein	.6g
Carbohydrate	.15g
Sugars	.14g
Fat	.15g
Saturates	.2g

INGREDIENTS

2 lb 4 oz/1 kg bok choy

about 3½ cups peanut oil

1 tsp salt

1 tbsp superfine sugar

generous ⅜ cup toasted pine nuts

cook's tip

The tough, outer leaves of bok choy are discarded as these will spoil the overall taste and texture of the dish. Use savoy cabbage instead of bok choy if it is unavailable.

1 Rinse the bok choy leaves under cold running water, then pat dry thoroughly with paper towels.

2 Discarding any tough outer leaves, roll each bok choy leaf up, then slice thinly so that the leaves are finely shredded. Alternatively, use a food processor to shred the bok choy.

3 Heat the peanut oil in a large preheated wok or heavy-bottom skillet. Carefully add the shredded bok choy and cook for 30 seconds, or until it shrivels up and becomes crispy. (You will probably need to do this in several batches.) Remove the crispy seaweed from the wok with a strainer and drain on paper towels.

4 Transfer the crispy seaweed to a large bowl, toss with the salt, sugar and pine nuts, and serve.

spicy corn fritters

serves 4   **prep: 5 mins** ⏲   **cook: 15 mins** ⏲

*Cornmeal can be found in most supermarkets or health food stores
—it is yellow in color. It acts as a binding agent in this recipe.*

INGREDIENTS

8 oz/225 g canned or frozen corn	2 tbsp chopped fresh cilantro
2 fresh red chiles, seeded and very finely chopped	1 large egg
2 garlic cloves, crushed	½ cup cornmeal
10 kaffir lime leaves, very finely chopped	3½ oz/100 g fine green beans, very finely sliced
	peanut oil, for cooking

variation

Add 1 tablespoon of Satay Sauce (see page 64) to the mixture in Step 1 for a slightly nuttier flavor.

cook's tip

Kaffir lime leaves are dark green, glossy leaves that have a lemony-lime flavor. They can be bought from specialist Asian stores either fresh or dried. Fresh leaves impart the most delicious flavor.

1 Place the corn, chiles, garlic, lime leaves, cilantro, egg, and cornmeal in a large mixing bowl and stir with a wooden spoon to combine. Add the green beans and mix well.

2 Divide the mixture into small, evenly sized balls.

Flatten the balls of mixture between the palms of your hands to form circles.

3 Heat a little peanut oil in a preheated wok or large skillet until very hot. Cook the fritters in the hot oil, in batches, until brown and crispy on the outside, turning

occasionally. Let each batch of fritters drain on paper towels while cooking the remainder.

4 Transfer the fritters to warmed serving plates and serve immediately.

thai golden pouches

cook: 10–15 mins   **prep: 10 mins**   **serves 4**

These crisp little "moneybags" are totally irresistible. Serve them as an appetizer or as canapés with pre-dinner drinks.

INGREDIENTS

4 oz/115 g crabmeat, thawed if frozen or drained if canned	1 egg, lightly beaten
	1 tbsp Thai fish sauce
½ cup fresh ground pork	1 tbsp dark soy sauce
2 oz/55 g fresh shiitake mushrooms, finely chopped	pinch of sugar
	pepper
1 tsp chopped fresh garlic	20 won ton skins
2 tbsp chopped scallions	oil, for deep frying
1 tbsp chopped fresh cilantro	Thai chili sauce, to serve

variation

If you cannot find the Thai chili sauce, then use Tabasco or a light sauce instead. Use peanut or vegetable oil for deep-frying the pouches.

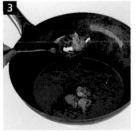

cook's tip

Won ton skins are paper-thin squares of dough made from flour and egg. They are available from supermarkets and Asian food stores. Thai chili sauce is also available from Asian food stores.

1 Mix the crabmeat, pork, mushrooms, garlic, scallions, cilantro, egg, fish sauce, soy sauce, and sugar together in a bowl and season to taste with pepper.

2 Place 1 teaspoon of the mixture in the center of a won ton skin. Fold up the edges and pinch the top together to seal. Fill the remaining skins in the same way.

3 Heat the oil in a preheated wok or large, heavy-bottom skillet. Add the won tons, in batches, and deep-fry until golden brown and crisp. Remove with a slotted spoon and drain on paper towels. Serve immediately with Thai chili sauce for dipping.

bruschetta

serves 4   prep: 10 mins ⏲   cook: 15 mins ⏲

These tasty little tomato and mozzarella cheese toasts can be served as finger food at a party and as an appetizer. Remember to switch on the broiler and oven to preheat before you start the preparation.

INGREDIENTS

2 small ciabatta loaves

¾ cup sun-dried tomato paste

10 oz/280 g mozzarella cheese, diced

1 tbsp chopped fresh oregano

pepper

2 tbsp olive oil

mixed salad greens, to serve

NUTRITIONAL INFORMATION	
Calories 578	
Protein 24g	
Carbohydrate 38g	
Sugars 2g	
Fat 37g	
Saturates 12g	

variation

If you cannot find fresh oregano, then use dried instead. Alternatively, use the same amount of chopped fresh basil.

1 Preheat the oven to 425°F/220°C and preheat the broiler to medium. Slice the bread diagonally, discarding the end crusts, to give a total of about 24 slices. Toast the bread lightly on both sides under the preheated broiler.

2 Spread the tomato paste evenly onto 1 side of each slice of toast, then top each with the diced mozzarella cheese.

3 Place the bruschetta on a large baking sheet and sprinkle with the oregano. Season to taste with pepper and drizzle with the olive oil. Bake in the preheated oven for 5 minutes, or until the mozzarella has melted.

Let stand for 2 minutes, then serve warm with mixed salad greens.

bacon with corn salad

⏱ **cook: 10 mins**   ⏱ **prep: 10 mins**   **serves 6**

Corn salad, also known as lamb's lettuce and mâche, although it is neither true lettuce nor corn, has a sweet flavor that is perfectly complemented by crispy bacon and garlic croutons.

NUTRITIONAL INFORMATION	
Calories	270
Protein	8g
Carbohydrate	9g
Sugars	1g
Fat	23g
Saturates	5g

INGREDIENTS

6–8 tbsp corn oil

8 oz/225 g rindless lean bacon, diced

2 garlic cloves, finely chopped

4 slices of white bread, crusts removed, cut into ½-inch/1-cm cubes

5 tbsp red wine vinegar

1 tbsp balsamic vinegar

2 tsp whole-grain mustard

salt and pepper

8 oz/225 g corn salad

cook's tip

If you buy corn salad with the root still attached, let it stand in a bowl of iced water for 1 hour to refresh (if you have time).

1 Heat 2 teaspoons of the corn oil in a large, heavy-bottom skillet. Add the bacon and cook over medium heat, stirring frequently, for 5 minutes, or until crisp. Remove from the skillet with a slotted spoon and drain on paper towels. Add the garlic and diced bread to the skillet and cook, stirring and tossing frequently, until crisp and golden brown on all sides. Remove from the skillet with a slotted spoon and drain on paper towels.

2 Place the red wine vinegar, balsamic vinegar, mustard, and remaining corn oil in a screw-top jar and shake vigorously, then pour into a bowl. Alternatively, mix the vinegars and mustard together in a bowl and whisk in the oil until the dressing is creamy. Season to taste with salt and pepper.

3 Add the corn salad and bacon to the dressing and toss to coat. Divide the salad between serving plates, sprinkle with the croutons, and serve.

chicken or beef satay

serves 6 **prep: 15 mins, plus 2 hrs marinating** ⏱ **cook: 15 mins** ⏱

*In this dish, strips of chicken or beef are threaded onto skewers,
broiled and served with a rich, spicy peanut sauce.*

INGREDIENTS

4 boneless, skinned chicken breasts or
1 lb 10 oz/750 g rump steak, trimmed

MARINADE

1 small onion, finely chopped
1 garlic clove, crushed
1-inch/2.5-cm piece fresh
gingerroot, grated
2 tbsp dark soy sauce
2 tsp chili powder
1 tsp ground coriander
2 tsp dark brown sugar
1 tbsp lemon or lime juice
1 tbsp vegetable oil

SATAY SAUCE

1¼ cups coconut milk
4 tbsp crunchy peanut butter
1 tbsp nam pla (Thai fish sauce)
1 tsp lemon or lime juice
salt and pepper

NUTRITIONAL INFORMATION	
Calories	.314
Protein	.32g
Carbohydrate	.10g
Sugars	.8g
Fat	.16g
Saturates	.4g

variation

If you don't want to make the Satay
Sauce yourself, try a store-bought
version—many supermarkets sell good,
ready-made dipping sauces.

cook's tip

If you don't have any bamboo
skewers, thin wooden skewers
will work just as well. Soak
them in cold water to prevent
them burning while the meat
is cooking.

1 Place 18 bamboo skewers in cold water to soak. Using a sharp knife, trim any fat from the meat, then cut it into thin strips, about 3-inches/7.5-cm long.

2 To make the marinade, place all the ingredients in a shallow dish and mix well. Add the meat strips and turn in the marinade until well coated. Cover with plastic wrap and let marinate in the refrigerator for 2 hours, or preferably overnight.

3 Preheat the broiler to medium. Remove the meat from the marinade and thread it, concertina style, onto the presoaked skewers.

4 Broil the meat satays for 8–10 minutes, turning and brushing occasionally with the marinade, until completely cooked through.

5 Meanwhile, to make the sauce, mix the coconut milk with the peanut butter, nam pla, and lemon juice in a pan. Bring to a boil and cook for 3 minutes. Season to taste with salt and pepper. Transfer the sauce to a serving bowl and serve with the cooked satays.

antipasto volente

serves 6   **prep: 15 mins** ⟳   **cook: 0 mins** ⟳

In Italy, antipasti are served as appetizers before the pasta course.
The title of this dish translates roughly as "take your pick."

INGREDIENTS

7 oz/200 g canned tuna in oil, drained
and flaked into chunks

115 g/4 oz canned sardines in
oil, drained

3½ oz/100 g canned anchovy fillets
in oil, drained

6 oz/175 g cooked shelled
shrimp, deveined

4 oz/115 g prosciutto, cut into strips

6 oz/175 g mozzarella cheese, sliced

13½ oz/390 g canned artichoke hearts,
drained and halved lengthwise

3 fresh figs, sliced

8 oz/225 g canned asparagus
spears, drained

4 oz/115 g smoked salmon, thinly sliced

salt and pepper

⅔ cup black olives

extra virgin olive oil, for drizzling

lemon wedges, to garnish

NUTRITIONAL INFORMATION

Calories	.378
Protein	.43g
Carbohydrate	.4g
Sugars	.3g
Fat	.22g
Saturates	.6g

variation

If you like, use the same amount of
fresh asparagus spears, instead of
canned. Steam or cook in boiling
water for 5–7 minutes, or until tender.

cook's tip

Prosciutto is an Italian, salt-
cured ham. The best-known
variety is Parma ham from
Parma, but other regions in
Italy produce their own, such
as San Daniele from Friuli.

1 Arrange the tuna, sardines, anchovies, shrimp, prosciutto, mozzarella cheese, artichoke hearts, and figs on a large serving platter.

2 Wrap 2–3 asparagus spears in each slice of smoked salmon and add to the platter. Season the antipasto to taste with salt and pepper.

3 Sprinkle the olives over the platter and drizzle with the olive oil. Garnish with lemon wedges, then serve immediately or cover with plastic wrap and let chill in the refrigerator until required, but bring to room temperature before serving.

hummus

serves 4   prep: 5 mins   cook: 0 mins

This mildly spicy Middle Eastern dip is easy to make and tastes much better than store-bought brands. Serve with crudités, such as cauliflower florets, carrot, celery, and red bell pepper sticks.

INGREDIENTS

15 oz/425 g canned chickpeas, drained and rinsed
½ cup sesame seed paste
3 garlic cloves
½ cup lemon juice
3–4 tbsp water
salt and pepper

TO GARNISH
1 tbsp olive oil
pinch of cayenne pepper
1 tbsp chopped fresh parsley
6 black olives

NUTRITIONAL INFORMATION

Calories 340

Protein 13g

Carbohydrate 17g

Sugars 1g

Fat 25g

Saturates 3g

cook's tip

Sesame seed paste is a thick, oily paste made from crushed toasted sesame seeds. It is available from most large supermarkets and health food stores.

1 Mix the chickpeas, sesame seed paste, garlic, and lemon juice together in a bowl and beat in enough water to make a smooth paste. Season to taste with salt and pepper. Alternatively, place the chickpeas, sesame seed paste, garlic, lemon juice, and 3 tablespoons of the water in a food processor, season to taste

with salt and pepper, and process until a smooth paste forms. If the mixture is too thick, add a little more water.

2 Transfer the hummus to a serving dish and make a shallow dip in the center with the back of a spoon. Pour the olive oil into the dip and sprinkle with cayenne pepper. Garnish with

the chopped parsley and olives. Serve immediately or cover with plastic wrap and store in the refrigerator until required.

guacamole

cook: 0 mins   **prep: 5 mins**   **serves 4**

Serve this ever-popular Mexican avocado dip with crudités (see opposite), crusty bread, or tortilla chips. A spoonful on plain broiled steak also makes a wonderful garnish.

NUTRITIONAL INFORMATION	
Calories	.245
Protein	.3g
Carbohydrate	.3g
Sugars	.1g
Fat	.25g
Saturates	.6g

INGREDIENTS

3 avocados

2 tbsp lime juice

1 tbsp sour cream

1 tbsp olive oil

½ tsp cayenne pepper

3 scallions, finely chopped

2 garlic cloves, finely chopped

salt

crusty bread, to serve

1 Halve and pit the avocados and, using a spoon, scoop the flesh into a bowl. Add the lime juice and mash coarsely with a fork.

2 Add the sour cream, olive oil, cayenne pepper, scallions, and garlic and season to taste with salt. Mash until thoroughly blended, but do not make the guacamole completely smooth.

3 Scoop the mixture into a serving bowl and serve immediately with crusty bread. Alternatively, cover tightly with plastic wrap and store in the refrigerator for up to 2 hours.

variation

Add 2 chopped fresh tomatoes to the mixture in Step 2 and replace the sour cream with plain yogurt, if you like.

vegetarian fajitas

cook: 20 mins **prep: 10 mins** **serves 6**

These tasty vegetable wraps should be served so hot that your guests can hear them sizzling as you bring them to the table.

INGREDIENTS

2 tbsp corn oil

2 onions, thinly sliced

2 garlic cloves, finely chopped

2 green bell peppers, seeded and sliced

2 red bell peppers, seeded and sliced

4 fresh green chiles, seeded and sliced

2 tsp chopped fresh cilantro

12 wheat tortillas

8 oz/225 g mushrooms, sliced

salt and pepper

variation

If you don't like dishes too spicy, use 2 fresh chiles instead of 4, or omit them. The fajitas are good served with plain yogurt or sour cream.

cook's tip

Always wash your hands thoroughly after handling chiles and avoid touching your lips or eyes. If you have sensitive skin, wear rubber gloves.

1 Heat the oil in a heavy-bottom skillet. Add the onions and garlic and cook over low heat, stirring occasionally, for 5 minutes, or until softened. Stir in the green and red bell peppers, chiles, and cilantro and cook, stirring occasionally, for 10 minutes.

2 Meanwhile, dry-fry the tortillas, one at a time, for 30 seconds on each side in a separate skillet. Alternatively, stack the tortillas and heat in a microwave oven according to the package instructions.

3 Add the mushrooms to the vegetable mixture and cook, stirring constantly, for 1 minute. Season to taste with salt and pepper. Divide the vegetables between the tortillas, roll up, and serve immediately.

cured meats with olives & tomatoes

serves 4　　　　　**prep: 10 mins** ↺　　　　　**cook: 5 mins** ⏲

This is a typical antipasto dish with cold cured meats, stuffed olives, fresh tomatoes, and the extra flavor of basil and balsamic vinegar.

INGREDIENTS

4 plum tomatoes

1 tbsp balsamic vinegar

salt and pepper

6 canned anchovy fillets, drained and rinsed

2 tbsp capers, drained and rinsed

¾ cup green olives, pitted

6 oz/175 g mixed cured meats, sliced

8 fresh basil leaves

1 tbsp extra virgin olive oil

crusty bread, to serve

NUTRITIONAL INFORMATION

Calories	.312
Protein	.12g
Carbohydrate	.2g
Sugars	.1g
Fat	.28g
Saturates	.1g

variation

If you like, you could add slivers of roasted red bell pepper or artichoke hearts soaked in olive oil to this dish.

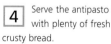

cook's tip

The cured meats for this recipe are up to your individual taste. They can include a selection of prosciutto, pancetta, bresaola (dried salt beef) and salame di Milano (pork and beef sausage).

1 Using a sharp knife, cut the tomatoes into evenly size slices. Sprinkle the tomato slices with the balsamic vinegar and a little salt and pepper to taste, and set aside.

2 Chop the anchovy fillets into pieces measuring about the same length as the olives. Carefully push a piece of anchovy and a caper into the center of each olive.

3 Arrange the sliced meat on 4 individual serving plates together with the tomatoes, stuffed olives, and basil leaves. Lightly drizzle the olive oil over the sliced meat, tomatoes, and olives.

4 Serve the antipasto with plenty of fresh crusty bread.

prosciutto & figs

serves 4   **prep: 5 mins** ⏲   **cook: 0 mins** ⏲

This classic Italian appetizer is simplicity itself, but never fails to please. It would be the perfect choice to start an alfresco meal. Find Parma ham or San Daniele as these are the finest prosciuttos.

INGREDIENTS

8 ripe fresh figs

8 thin slices of prosciutto, about 6 oz/175 g

pepper

NUTRITIONAL INFORMATION	
Calories 145	
Protein 13g	
Carbohydrate 10g	
Sugars 10g	
Fat 6g	
Saturates 2g	

1 Using a sharp knife, cut each fig downward into quarters from the stalk end, but without cutting all the way through. Gently open out each fruit like a flower and place 2 on each of 4 large serving plates.

2 Arrange 2 slices of prosciutto in decorative folds beside the figs on each plate.

3 Season well with pepper and serve at room temperature, offering the pepper shaker at the same time.

---

variation

Arrange 2 slices of prosciutto on each plate and sprinkle with Parmesan cheese shavings. Add 6 olives and drizzle with Vinaigrette (see page 13).

mozzarella & tomatoes

⏱ **cook: 0 mins**   ⏱ **prep: 5 mins**   **serves 4**

Known as insalata tricolore in Italy, this attractive and tasty appetizer deserves the best ingredients. Try to obtain mozzarella di bufala, *the genuine cheese made from water buffalo milk.*

NUTRITIONAL INFORMATION	
Calories	.446
Protein	.20g
Carbohydrate	.5g
Sugars	.5g
Fat	.39g
Saturates	.13g

INGREDIENTS

1 lb 5 oz/600 g plum tomatoes

10½ oz/300 g mozzarella cheese

16 fresh basil leaves, torn if large

½ cup extra virgin olive oil, to serve

1 Using a sharp knife, cut the tomatoes into even slices about ¼ inch/5 mm thick. Drain the mozzarella cheese and discard the whey. Slice the mozzarella cheese evenly.

2 Arrange the tomato and mozzarella slices, overlapping slightly, in concentric circles on a large serving plate.

3 Sprinkle the basil over the salad and serve immediately with the olive oil for drizzling.

cook's tip

If you can find them, use fresh plum tomatoes as they are less watery than the standard round varieties. Try to use sun-ripened tomatoes as they have a richer flavor.

sesame ginger chicken

serves 4 **prep: 15 mins, plus 2 hrs marinating** **cook: 10 mins**

Chunks of chicken breast are marinated in a mixture of lime juice, garlic, sesame oil, and fresh ginger to give them a great flavor.

INGREDIENTS

1 lb 2 oz/500 g boneless
chicken breasts

fresh mint sprigs, to garnish

MARINADE

1 garlic clove, crushed

1 shallot, very finely chopped

2 tbsp sesame oil

1 tbsp nam pla (Thai fish sauce) or
light soy sauce

finely grated rind of 1 lime or ½ lemon
and 2 tbsp lime or lemon juice

1 tsp sesame seeds

2 tsp finely grated fresh gingerroot

2 tsp chopped fresh mint

salt and pepper

NUTRITIONAL INFORMATION

Calories	.204
Protein	.28g
Carbohydrate	.1g
Sugars	.0g
Fat	.10g
Saturates	.2g

variation

If you prefer, substitute fresh cilantro for the fresh mint in this recipe, for a slightly mellower taste.

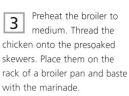

cook's tip

The kabobs taste delicious if dipped into an accompanying bowl of hot chili sauce. Many major supermarkets stock a variety of suitable ready-made dipping sauces.

1 Place 4 long skewers in cold water to soak. To make the marinade, place the garlic, shallot, sesame oil, nam pla, lime rind and juice, sesame seeds, gingerroot, and chopped mint into a large, nonmetallic bowl. Season with a little salt and pepper and mix together thoroughly.

2 Remove the skin from the chicken breasts and cut the flesh into chunks. Add the chicken to the marinade, stirring to coat completely in the mixture. Cover with plastic wrap and let chill in the refrigerator for at least 2 hours, so that the flavors are absorbed.

3 Preheat the broiler to medium. Thread the chicken onto the presoaked skewers. Place them on the rack of a broiler pan and baste with the marinade.

4 Place the kabobs under the preheated broiler for 8–10 minutes, turning

frequently and basting with the remaining marinade, until the meat is cooked through.

5 Serve the chicken skewers garnished with fresh mint sprigs.

salads & snacks

The busier the lifestyle, the more important it is to eat a healthy and balanced diet, yet all too often we dash home, grab a bag of potato chips, a canned fizzy drink, and a chocolate bar before flying out the door again or collapsing in an exhausted heap in front of the television. With only marginally more effort and time, you can prepare tasty and nourishing snacks for just those occasions when you don't feel like eating a whole meal, but you know that your body is craving some nourishment. Salads are the perfect choice when cooking is too much trouble or the weather is hot. Why settle for a limp lettuce leaf and piece of dried-up cheese, when, in next to no time, you can rustle up Greek Salad (see page 87) with feta, tomatoes, and olives or Caesar Salad (see page 85) with anchovies, croûtons, and a unique egg dressing?

A hot snack is just as easy. If you suddenly find yourself entertaining unexpected guests, try Pantry Tuna (see page 111); if you need a speedy weekend lunch before the family disperses for the afternoon's activities, serve Spaghetti alla Carbonara (see page 100); if it's too late for breakfast and too early for lunch, Eggs Benedict (see page 114) is the answer; or if you need to fire-up some energy before tackling the Christmas shopping, tuck into a plate of Caribbean Cook-Up Rice (see page 103).

salade niçoise

cook: 13–17 mins　　　**prep: 12–15 mins**　　　**serves 4**

This Provençal dish is probably the best-known and best-loved classic salad in the Western world. The combination of beans, tuna, tomatoes, and olives is virtually irresistible.

INGREDIENTS

2 eggs

12 small new potatoes

salt

4 oz/115 g green beans

2 romaine lettuces or 3 Boston lettuces

7 oz/200 g canned tuna in oil

6 canned anchovy fillets

4 tomatoes

4 scallions

12 black olives

2 tbsp bottled capers, drained

2 tbsp pine nuts

DRESSING

6 tbsp extra virgin olive oil

2 tbsp tarragon vinegar

1 tsp Dijon mustard

1 garlic clove, finely chopped

variation

Use fresh tuna instead of canned. Oil both sides of 2 tuna steaks and cook in a grill pan for 1–2 minutes. Slice and add to the salad in Step 3.

cook's tip

There are lots of different herb vinegars available in most large supermarkets, but if you cannot find tarragon vinegar, then use the same amount of white wine vinegar instead.

1 Cook the eggs, potatoes, and beans simultaneously. Place the eggs in a pan and cover with cold water. Bring to a boil, then reduce the heat and boil gently for 12 minutes. Cook the potatoes in a pan of lightly salted boiling water for 12–15 minutes, or until tender, and cook the green beans in a separate pan of lightly salted boiling water for 3–5 minutes.

2 Meanwhile, prepare all the remaining ingredients. Coarsely chop the lettuces, drain and flake the tuna, then drain the anchovies and halve them lengthwise. Chop the tomatoes and slice the scallions. To make the dressing, place all the ingredients in a large salad bowl and beat well to mix.

3 Drain the beans and refresh in cold water. Add to the salad bowl with the lettuces, tuna, anchovies, tomatoes, scallions, olives, and capers. Drain the eggs, cool under cold running water and set aside. Drain the potatoes and add to the salad. Lightly toast the pine nuts in a dry skillet, shaking the skillet frequently, for 1–2 minutes, or until golden. Sprinkle them over the salad. Shell and chop the eggs and add them to the salad.

4 Whisk the dressing again, add it to the salad, toss to coat, and serve.

mexican tomato salad

serves 4   **prep: 5 mins** ◔   **cook: 0 mins** ⏲

This easy and economical salad would make an ideal light vegetarian lunch, served with some crusty bread, or be a good accompaniment to a barbecue.

INGREDIENTS

1 lb 5 oz/600 g tomatoes, peeled, seeded, and coarsely chopped

1 onion, thinly sliced and pushed out into rings

14 oz/400 g canned kidney beans, drained and rinsed

1 fresh green chile, seeded and thinly sliced

3 tbsp chopped fresh cilantro

3 tbsp olive oil

1 garlic clove, finely chopped

4 tbsp lime juice

salt and pepper

NUTRITIONAL INFORMATION	
Calories	.210
Protein	.8g
Carbohydrate	.25g
Sugars	.10g
Fat	.9g
Saturates	.1g

variation

You could substitute two canned chipotle chiles, drained and rinsed, for the fresh chile, and fava beans for the kidney beans, if you prefer.

cook's tip

If this salad has been made in advance and stored in the refrigerator, then bring it back to room temperature before serving.

1 Place the chopped tomatoes and onion slices into a large serving bowl and mix well. Stir in the kidney beans.

2 Mix the chile, cilantro, olive oil, garlic, and lime juice together in a measuring cup and season to taste with salt and pepper.

3 Pour the dressing over the salad and toss thoroughly. Serve immediately or cover with plastic wrap and let chill in the refrigerator until required.

caesar salad

cook: 6 mins   **prep: 5–10 mins**   **serves 4**

NUTRITIONAL INFORMATION

Calories	.506
Protein	.16g
Carbohydrate	.26g
Sugars	.2g
Fat	.38g
Saturates	.9g

variation

Replace the romaine and Boston lettuces with mixed salad greens, such as lollo rosso, oak leaf, and arugula.

Created by Caesar Cardini in the 1920s, the classic version of this salad includes raw egg in the dressing, but in this recipe, the egg is very lightly cooked first.

INGREDIENTS

⅔ cup olive oil	2 tbsp lemon juice
2 garlic cloves	salt and pepper
5 slices white bread, crusts removed, cut into ½-inch/1-cm cubes	8 canned anchovy fillets, drained and coarsely chopped
1 large egg	¾ cup fresh Parmesan cheese shavings
2 romaine lettuces or 3 Boston lettuces	

cook's tip

Don't leave the salad standing round too long after the dressing has been added or the lettuce will go soggy and the salad will be unusable.

 1 Bring a small, heavy-bottom pan of water to a boil.

2 Meanwhile, heat 4 tablespoons of the olive oil in a heavy-bottom skillet. Add the garlic and diced bread and cook, stirring and tossing frequently, for 4–5 minutes, or until the bread is crispy and golden all over.

Remove from the skillet with a slotted spoon and drain on paper towels.

3 Add the egg to the boiling water and cook for 1 minute, then remove from the pan and set aside.

4 Arrange the lettuce leaves in a salad bowl. Mix the remaining olive oil and lemon juice together, then season to taste with salt and pepper. Crack the egg into the dressing and whisk to blend. Pour the dressing over the lettuce leaves, toss well, then add the croutons and anchovies and toss the salad again. Sprinkle with Parmesan cheese shavings and serve.

chef's salad

The name of the chef responsible for this substantial salad with its piquant Thousand Island Dressing seems to be lost in the mists of time—but he was clearly a good chap.

INGREDIENTS

1 iceberg lettuce, shredded

6 oz/175 g cooked ham, cut into thin strips

6 oz/175 g cooked tongue, cut into thin strips

12 oz/350 g cooked chicken, cut into thin strips

6 oz/175 g Swiss cheese

4 tomatoes, quartered

3 hard-cooked eggs, shelled and quartered

1¾ cups Thousand Island Dressing (see page 13)

NUTRITIONAL INFORMATION

Calories	730
Protein	. . . . .41g
Carbohydrate	. . . . .5g
Sugars	. . . . .5g
Fat	. . . . .61g
Saturates	. . . . .15g

1　Arrange the lettuce on a large serving platter. Arrange the cold meat decoratively on top.

2　Cut the Swiss cheese into thin sticks, sprinkle over the salad, and arrange the tomato and egg quarters round the edge of the platter.

3　Serve the salad immediately, handing the dressing separately.

cook's tip

This is a good salad to take on a picnic. Pack the salad in a large rigid container and pack the dressing in a separate covered bowl, then serve the salad and dressing separately.

greek salad

cook: 0 mins　　　　**prep: 10 mins**　　　　**serves 4**

As you might expect, this is the perfect salad for a very hot day, as the piquancy of the feta cheese contrasts with the refreshing cucumber, succulent tomatoes, and fruity olives.

NUTRITIONAL INFORMATION

Calories 373

Protein 17g

Carbohydrate 2g

Sugars . . . . ?g

Fat 33g

Saturates 2g

INGREDIENTS

1 cucumber, halved lengthwise

18 cherry tomatoes, halved

14 oz/400 g feta cheese

4 tbsp extra virgin olive oil

1 tbsp lemon juice

12 black olives

salt and pepper

ciabatta bread, to serve

cook's tip

Although originally made from ewe's milk, much modern feta is now made from cow's milk. It is worth looking for the genuine cheese, made either in Greece or Bulgaria.

1 Using a sharp knife, cut the cucumber halves into ½-inch/1-cm thick slices and divide between 4 individual serving plates with the cherry tomatoes.

2 Crumble the feta cheese over the salads and drizzle with the olive oil and lemon juice.

3 Sprinkle the olives over the salads and season to taste with salt and pepper, but bear in mind that both the olives and the feta will be quite salty. Toss lightly and serve with ciabatta.

russian salad

serves 4   prep: 10 mins   cook: 20 mins

Created in France for aristocrats who had fled the Russian revolution, the recipe for this salad has itself undergone some dramatic changes over the years.

INGREDIENTS

4 oz/115 g new potatoes

generous 1 cup frozen or shelled fresh fava beans

4 oz/115 g baby carrots

4 oz/115 g baby corn

4 oz/115 g baby turnips

4 oz/115 g white mushrooms, cut into thin sticks

12 oz/350 g cooked shelled shrimp, deveined

½ cup mayonnaise

1 tbsp lemon juice

2 tbsp bottled capers, drained and rinsed

salt and pepper

2 tbsp extra virgin olive oil

2 hard-cooked eggs, shelled and halved

4 canned anchovy fillets, drained and halved

paprika, to garnish

NUTRITIONAL INFORMATION	
Calories	512
Protein	32g
Carbohydrate	13g
Sugars	5g
Fat	37g
Saturates	6g

variation

Replace the white mushrooms with the same amount of cremini mushrooms, if you prefer.

cook's tip

If you find canned anchovies too salty, then place them in a small bowl and cover with milk. Let soak for 10 minutes, then drain and pat dry with paper towels.

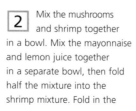

1 Cook the new potatoes, fava beans, carrots, corn, and turnips simultaneously. Cook the potatoes in a large, heavy-bottom pan of lightly salted boiling water for 20 minutes. Cook the fava beans in a small pan of lightly salted water for 3 minutes, then drain, refresh under cold running water and set aside until required. Cook the carrots, corn, and turnips in a large, heavy-bottom pan of lightly salted boiling water for 6 minutes.

2 Mix the mushrooms and shrimp together in a bowl. Mix the mayonnaise and lemon juice together in a separate bowl, then fold half the mixture into the shrimp mixture. Fold in the capers and season to taste with salt and pepper.

3 Drain the mixed vegetables, refresh under cold running water and tip into a bowl. When the potatoes are cooked, drain, refresh under cold running water and tip into the bowl. Pop the fava beans out of their skins by pinching them between your index finger and thumb and add to the bowl. Add the olive oil and toss to coat. Divide the potatoes and vegetables between serving plates and top with the shrimp mixture. Place a hard-cooked egg half in the center of each and decorate with the halved anchovies. Dust the eggs with paprika and serve with the remaining mayonnaise mixture.

lentil pâté

serves 4 **prep: 30 mins, plus 1 hr chilling** **cook: 1 hr 15 mins**

Red lentils are used in this spicy recipe for speed because they do not require any presoaking. The pâté makes a tasty and unusual appetizer for a vegetarian dinner party.

INGREDIENTS

1 tbsp vegetable oil, plus extra for greasing

1 onion, chopped

2 garlic cloves, crushed

1 tsp garam masala

½ tsp ground coriander

3½ cups Vegetable Stock (see page 13)

scant ⅞ cup split red lentils

1 small egg

2 tbsp milk

2 tbsp mango chutney

2 tbsp chopped fresh parsley

fresh parsley sprigs, to garnish

TO SERVE

salad greens

toast

NUTRITIONAL INFORMATION

Calories 267

Protein 14g

Carbohydrate 37g

Sugars 12g

Fat 8g

Saturates 1g

variation

You can use other types of lentils, such as Puy lentils, for this recipe, but you will need to include soaking time in your preparations.

cook's tip

It is always better to make your own stock, if you can find the time, rather than use stock cubes, because the flavor of homemade stock is far superior.

1 Preheat the oven to 400°F/200°C. Heat the oil in a large pan and sauté the onion and garlic, stirring constantly, for 2–3 minutes. Add the spices and cook for an additional 30 seconds. Stir in the Stock and lentils and bring the mixture to a boil. Reduce the heat and let

simmer for 20 minutes, until the lentils are cooked and softened. Remove the pan from the heat and drain off any excess moisture.

2 Place the mixture in a food processor and add the egg, milk, chutney, and parsley. Process until smooth.

3 Grease and line the bottom of a 1-lb/450-g loaf pan and spoon in the mixture, smoothing the surface. Cover and cook in the oven for 40–45 minutes, or until firm to the touch.

4 Let cool in the pan for 20 minutes, then chill in the refrigerator for 1 hour.

5 Turn out the pâté onto a serving plate, slice and garnish with fresh parsley. Serve with salad greens and lightly cooked toast.

smoked fish & potato pâté

serves 4   **prep: 20 mins** 🕐   **cook: 10 mins** 🕐

This smoked fish pâté is given a tart, fruity flavor by fresh gooseberries, which complement the fish perfectly.

INGREDIENTS

1 lb 7 oz/650 g floury potatoes, diced

10½ oz/300 g smoked mackerel, skinned and flaked

2¾ oz/75 g cooked gooseberries

2 tsp lemon juice

2 tbsp low fat sour cream

1 tbsp capers

1 gherkin, chopped

1 tbsp chopped dill pickle

1 tbsp chopped fresh dill

salt and pepper

lemon wedges, to garnish

toast or warm crusty bread, to serve

NUTRITIONAL INFORMATION

Calories 418

Protein 18g

Carbohydrate 32g

Sugars 4g

Fat 25g

Saturates 6g

variation

Add a slightly different flavor to the pâté by using chopped fresh parsley or snipped chives instead of the fresh dill.

cook's tip

Use stewed, canned, or bottled cooked gooseberries for convenience and to save time, or when fresh gooseberries are out of season.

1 Cook the potatoes in a pan of boiling water for 10 minutes, or until tender, then drain well.

2 Place the cooked potatoes in a food processor or blender, add the smoked mackerel, and process for 30 seconds, or until fairly smooth. Alternatively, place the ingredients in a bowl and mash with a fork.

3 Add the cooked gooseberries, lemon juice, and sour cream to the fish and potato mixture. Blend for an additional 10 seconds, or mash well.

4 Stir in the capers, gherkin, dill pickle, and dill. Season well with salt and pepper.

5 Turn the fish pâté into a serving dish, garnish with lemon wedges, and serve with slices of toast or chunks of warm crusty bread.

shallots à la grecque

serves 4 **prep: 10 mins** **cook: 15 mins**

This is a well-known method of cooking vegetables using olive oil, honey, and wine, and tastes perfect served with a crisp salad.

INGREDIENTS

1 lb/450 g shallots

3 tbsp olive oil

3 tbsp honey

2 tbsp garlic wine vinegar

3 tbsp dry white wine

1 tbsp tomato paste

2 celery stalks, sliced

2 tomatoes, seeded and chopped

salt and pepper

chopped celery leaves, to garnish

NUTRITIONAL INFORMATION

Calories 200

Protein 2g

Carbohydrate 28g

Sugars 26g

Fat 9g

Saturates 1g

1 Peel the shallots. Heat the oil in a large pan, add the shallots, and cook, stirring, for 3–5 minutes, or until they start to brown.

2 Add the honey and cook over high heat for an additional 30 seconds, then add the garlic wine vinegar and white wine, stirring well.

3 Stir in the tomato paste, celery, and tomatoes and bring the mixture to a boil. Cook over high heat for 5–6 minutes. Season to taste and let cool slightly.

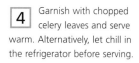

4 Garnish with chopped celery leaves and serve warm. Alternatively, let chill in the refrigerator before serving.

variation

You can substitute the shallots with small onions or onion wedges, which taste just as good cooked à la Grecque.

baked fennel

cook: 35 mins   **prep: 10 mins**   **serves 4**

Fennel is used extensively in northern Italy. It is a very versatile vegetable, which is good cooked or used raw in salads.

NUTRITIONAL INFORMATION

Calories	111
Protein	. . . . .7g
Carbohydrate	. . . . .7g
Sugars	. . . . .6g
Fat	. . . . .7g
Saturates	. . . . .3g

INGREDIENTS

2 fennel bulbs

2 celery stalks, cut into 3-inch/

7.5-cm lengths

6 sun-dried tomatoes, halved

7 oz/200 g strained tomatoes

2 tsp dried oregano

generous ¾ cup freshly grated

Parmesan cheese, plus extra to garnish

crusty bread, to serve (optional)

variation

Sprinkle pine nuts over the dish before serving to add a little protein and extra flavor.

1 Preheat the oven to 375°F/190°C. Using a sharp knife, trim the fennel, discarding any tough outer leaves, and cut the bulb into quarters.

2 Bring a large pan of water to a boil, add the fennel and celery, and cook for 8–10 minutes, or until just tender. Remove with a slotted spoon and drain.

3 Place the fennel pieces, celery, and sun-dried tomatoes in an ovenproof dish. Mix the strained tomatoes with the oregano and pour the mixture over the fennel.

4 Sprinkle with the Parmesan cheese and bake in the preheated oven for 20 minutes, or until piping hot. Serve as an appetizer with crusty bread, or as a vegetable side dish, garnished with Parmesan cheese shavings.

chicken goujons

cook: 15 mins   **prep: 15 mins**   **serves 4**

NUTRITIONAL INFORMATION	
Calories	.655
Protein	.36g
Carbohydrate	.48g
Sugars	.3g
Fat	.37g
Saturates	.16g

variation

Instead of the cheese & chive dip, serve the goujons with Guacamole (see page 69), Thousand Island Dressing (see page 13), or just mayonnaise.

Popular with adults and children alike, these tasty strips of chicken would make a good lunch served with salad and new potatoes or, equally, could be served on their own as an appetizer for six.

INGREDIENTS

4 skinless, boneless chicken breasts, about 4 oz/115 g each

3 tbsp all-purpose flour

corn oil, for deep-frying

1½ cups dried bread crumbs

1 tsp ground coriander

2 tsp paprika

salt and pepper

2 eggs, lightly beaten

CHEESE & CHIVE DIP

½ cup cream cheese

⅔ cup sour cream

3 tbsp chopped fresh chives

salt and pepper

paprika, for sprinkling

TO GARNISH

lemon wedges

fresh chives

cook's tip

When deep-frying, make sure that the oil is at the correct temperature before cooking. If it is too hot it will burn the food on the outside, but leave the inside raw.

1 Place the chicken breasts between 2 sheets of plastic wrap and beat with the flat side of a meat mallet or with the side of a rolling pin until ¼-inch/5-mm thick. Slice diagonally into 1-inch/2.5-cm strips. Place the flour in a plastic bag and add the chicken strips, a few at a time, shaking well until the chicken is coated.

2 Heat the corn oil in a large, heavy-bottom pan to 350–375°F/180–190°C, or until a cube of bread browns in 30 seconds. Meanwhile, mix the bread crumbs, coriander, and paprika together, season to taste with salt and pepper, and spread out on a plate. Dip the chicken strips first in the beaten egg and then in the bread crumb

mixture. When the oil is hot, deep-fry the goujons, in batches, until crisp and golden all over. Remove from the pan with a slotted spoon and drain on paper towels.

3 Meanwhile, make the dip. Mix the cream cheese, sour cream, and chives together in a serving bowl, season to taste with salt and

pepper, and sprinkle with paprika. Transfer the goujons to a large serving plate and garnish with lemon wedges. Garnish the dip with chives and serve with the goujons.

deep-fried seafood

serves 4   **prep: 5 mins** ⦿   **cook: 15 mins** ⦿

Deep-fried seafood is a popular dish all round the Mediterranean, where fish of every shape and flavor is fresh and abundant.

INGREDIENTS

7 oz/200 g prepared squid

7 oz/200 g jumbo shrimp, shelled and deveined

5½ oz/150 g smelt

oil, for deep-frying

generous ¼ cup all-purpose flour

1 tsp dried basil

salt and pepper

TO SERVE

garlic mayonnaise

lemon wedges

NUTRITIONAL INFORMATION	
Calories	.393
Protein	.27g
Carbohydrate	.12g
Sugars	.0.2g
Fat	.26g
Saturates	.3g

variation

To give this dish more of an Eastern flavor, try serving the deep-fried seafood with chili sauce and lime wedges.

1 Rinse the squid, shrimp, and smelt under cold running water to remove any dirt or grit. Using a sharp knife, slice the squid into rings, leaving the tentacles whole.

2 Heat the oil in a large pan to 350–375°F/180–190°C, or until a cube of bread browns in 30 seconds.

3 Place the flour in a bowl, add the basil and season to taste with salt and pepper. Mix well. Roll the squid, shrimp, and smelt in the seasoned flour until coated. Shake off any excess flour.

4 Cook the seafood in the hot oil, in batches, for 2–3 minutes, or until crispy and golden all over. Remove all of the seafood with a slotted spoon and let drain thoroughly on paper towels.

5 Transfer the seafood to serving plates and serve with garlic mayonnaise and a few lemon wedges.

eggplant dipping platter

⏲ **cook: 10 mins**   ⏱ **prep: 15 mins**   **serves 4**

Dipping platters are healthy and delicious—great for informal occasions, or for serving with drinks before dinner.

NUTRITIONAL INFORMATION	
Calories	.81
Protein	.4g
Carbohydrate	.5g
Sugars	.4g
Fat	.5g
Saturates	.1g

INGREDIENTS

1 eggplant

3 tbsp sesame seeds

1 tsp sesame oil

grated rind and juice of ½ lime

1 small shallot, diced

salt and pepper

1 tsp sugar

1 fresh red chile, seeded and sliced

4½ oz/125 g broccoli florets

2 carrots, cut into short thin sticks

8 baby corn, halved lengthwise

2 celery stalks, cut into short thin sticks

1 baby red cabbage, cut into 8 wedges

variation

You can vary the selection of vegetables, depending on your preference. Other vegetables you could use include cauliflower florets and cucumber sticks.

1 Peel the eggplant and cut the flesh into 1-inch/2.5-cm cubes. Cook in a pan of boiling water for 7–8 minutes.

2 Meanwhile, place the sesame seeds in a dry pan over low heat and roast for 1–2 minutes, until golden. Place the sesame seeds in a food processor with the oil and blend, or crush them with the oil using a mortar and pestle.

3 Add the eggplant, lime rind and juice, shallot, ½ teaspoon of salt, pepper, sugar, and chile in that order to the sesame seeds. Process, or chop and mash by hand, until smooth. Adjust the seasoning to taste, then spoon the dip into a bowl.

4 Serve the dipping platter surrounded by the broccoli, carrots, baby corn, celery, and red cabbage.

spaghetti alla carbonara

serves 4   **prep: 10 mins** ⟳   **cook: 10 mins** ⟳

This is one of the quickest, simplest, most economical and tastiest of pasta dishes. It is not difficult to cook, but it is important to keep everything really hot so that the egg cooks lightly when it is added at the end, but doesn't scramble.

INGREDIENTS

1 lb/450 g dried spaghetti

6 oz/175 g rindless lean bacon, diced

1 garlic clove, finely chopped

3 eggs, lightly beaten

salt and pepper

4 tbsp fresh Parmesan cheese shavings

NUTRITIONAL INFORMATION	
Calories 607	
Protein 29g	
Carbohydrate 84g	
Sugars 4g	
Fat 29g	
Saturates 20g	

variation

For additional flavor, you could add 2 cups sliced white or cremini mushrooms to the skillet in Step 2.

cook's tip

It is best to buy fresh Parmesan cheese, available in most supermarkets in a block, and grate or shave it yourself, as it tastes much better than ready-grated Parmesan cheese.

1 Bring a large, heavy-bottom pan of lightly salted water to a boil. Add the pasta, return to a boil and cook for 8–10 minutes, or until tender but still firm to the bite.

2 Meanwhile, cook the bacon and garlic in a large, heavy-bottom, dry skillet over medium heat for 5 minutes, or until the bacon is crisp-tender. Remove from the skillet and drain on paper towels.

3 Drain the pasta and return it to the pan, but do not return to the heat. Add the bacon and garlic and the eggs. Season to taste with salt and pepper. Toss thoroughly with 2 large forks. Add half the Parmesan cheese and toss again. Transfer to a warmed serving dish, sprinkle with the remaining Parmesan cheese, and serve immediately.

caribbean cook-up rice

cook: 25 mins   **prep: 5 mins**   **serves 4**

NUTRITIONAL INFORMATION

Calories 674

Protein 16g

Carbohydrate 118g

Sugars 5g

Fat 19g

Saturates 12g

variation

While not authentic, you could substitute canned chickpeas if gunga peas are not available.

Gunga peas, also known as gungo, pigeon, and Jamaica peas, are popular in Africa, India and, most of all, in the Caribbean. They have a nutty flavor, more like a bean than a pea.

INGREDIENTS

2 tbsp butter

1 onion, chopped

1 garlic clove, finely chopped

1 carrot, chopped

14 oz/400 g canned gunga peas, drained and rinsed

1 cinnamon stick

1 fresh thyme sprig

2½ cups Vegetable Stock (see page 13)

2 oz/55 g block creamed coconut

1 fresh green chile, seeded and chopped

salt and pepper

scant 2 cups long-grain rice

cook's tip

When cooking with rice, especially long-grain and basmati, always rinse it under cold running water first as this removes all the excess starch.

1 Melt the butter in a large, heavy-bottom skillet or flameproof casserole. Add the onion and garlic and cook over low heat, stirring occasionally, for 5 minutes, or until softened.

2 Add the carrot, gunga peas, cinnamon stick, thyme, Vegetable Stock, coconut, and chile, stir well, and season to taste with salt and pepper. Bring to a boil, stirring frequently.

3 Add the rice and return to a boil, then reduce the heat, cover, and let simmer for 15 minutes, or until the rice is tender and all the liquid has been absorbed. Remove and discard the thyme sprig and cinnamon stick, then fluff up the rice with a fork. Transfer to individual serving dishes and serve immediately.

speedy vegetable pilau

serves 4 **prep: 5 mins** **cook: 15–20 mins**

You can serve this tasty rice dish as a filling, vegetarian snack or as an accompaniment to meat or fish, in which case, this quantity would serve six people.

INGREDIENTS

scant 2 cups basmati rice

2 tbsp corn oil

2 garlic cloves, finely chopped

½ cinnamon stick

2 cardamom pods

½ tsp black cumin seeds

1 tomato, sliced

2 oz/55 g baby white mushrooms

generous ½ cup shelled peas

3 cups Vegetable Stock

(see page 13)

NUTRITIONAL INFORMATION

Calories 474

Protein 10g

Carbohydrate 93g

Sugars 1g

Fat 6g

Saturates 1g

---

variation

Use the same amount of sliced cremini mushrooms instead of the white ones and if shelled peas are not available, then use frozen instead.

cook's tip

If you have time, soak the rice in a large bowl of cold water for 10 minutes before cooking, as this helps to lighten the grain.

1 Rinse the basmati rice thoroughly in 2–3 changes of water, drain well, and set aside until required.

2 Heat the corn oil in a large, heavy-bottom pan or flameproof casserole. Add the garlic, cinnamon stick, cardamom, and cumin, and cook, stirring constantly, for 1 minute. Add the tomato and mushrooms and cook, stirring constantly, for 3 minutes.

3 Stir in the rice and peas and cook for 1 minute, stirring to coat the grains, then add the Vegetable Stock and bring to a boil. Reduce the heat, cover, and let simmer for 10–15 minutes, or until the rice is tender and the liquid has been absorbed. Remove and discard the cinnamon stick and serve immediately.

singapore noodles

⏱ **cook: 5 mins**

🕐 **prep: 5 mins, plus 10 mins soaking**

serves 4

NUTRITIONAL INFORMATION	
Calories	.430
Protein	.27g
Carbohydrate	.38g
Sugars	.1g
Fat	.18g
Saturates	.4g

variation

Replace the pork and chicken sticks with the same amount of cooked ground pork and chicken. Use a red bell pepper instead of a green pepper.

This spicy noodle dish is easily adapted to include whatever you have to hand—you could substitute Thai fish cakes for the shrimp, for example. Save time by cutting up the meat and vegetables while the noodles are soaking.

INGREDIENTS

6 oz/175 g rice noodles

5 tbsp peanut oil

salt

2 scallions, sliced

3 oz/85 g cooked shelled shrimp

6 oz/175 g cooked pork, cut into thin sticks

3 oz/85 g cooked chicken, cut into thin sticks

1 green bell pepper, seeded and cut into thin sticks

½ tsp sugar

2 tsp curry powder

2 tsp dark soy sauce

cook's tip

Dark soy sauce is darker, sweeter and stronger than light soy sauce. It goes well with meat dishes containing beef, pork, or duck.

1 Place the noodles in a large bowl and pour over enough warm water to cover. Let soak for 10 minutes, or according to the package instructions. Drain well and pat dry with paper towels. Heat half the peanut oil in a preheated wok or large, heavy-bottom skillet. Add the soaked noodles and a pinch of salt and stir-fry for 2 minutes. Transfer to a heatproof bowl with a slotted spoon and keep warm.

2 Add the remaining peanut oil to the wok or skillet. When it is hot, add the sliced scallions, cooked shrimp, pork sticks, chicken sticks, green bell pepper sticks, sugar, curry powder, and a pinch of salt, and stir-fry for 1 minute.

3 Return the noodles to the wok or skillet and stir-fry, tossing the ingredients together, for an additional 2 minutes. Stir in the soy sauce and serve.

cheese fritters

serves 4　　　　　**prep: 10 mins** ◔　　　　　**cook: 15 mins** ♨

These crisp little snacks can be served at any time of day and make lovely, hot nibbles for a party.

INGREDIENTS

1 cup cream cheese

⅜ cup all-purpose flour

2 large potatoes, grated

1 egg, lightly beaten

generous ¼–½ cup milk

salt and pepper

corn oil, for cooking

NUTRITIONAL INFORMATION

Calories 467

Protein 7g

Carbohydrate 27g

Sugars 2g

Fat 38g

Saturates 19g

1 Beat the cream cheese in a bowl until it is smooth and soft. Sift the flour into a separate bowl and fold in the cream cheese. Beat in the grated potatoes, egg, and enough milk to make a smooth, thick batter. Season to taste with salt and pepper.

2 Pour the corn oil into a heavy-bottom skillet to a depth of 1 inch/2.5 cm and heat. Add spoonfuls of the batter to the skillet, spacing them well apart, and cook for 2–3 minutes on each side, or until golden brown.

3 Remove from the skillet with a spatula and drain on paper towels. Keep warm while you cook the remaining fritters, then serve immediately.

cook's tip

You can also cook these tasty cheese fritters in a deep-fryer for 2–4 minutes and serve with a hot chili sauce or plain mayonnaise for dipping.

cheese aigrettes

cook: 20 mins   **prep: 10 mins**   **serves 6**

Light-as-air, choux puffs are deep-fried to make these sensational cheese snacks—perfect party food.

NUTRITIONAL INFORMATION

Calories	354
Protein	. . . . .12g
Carbohydrate	. . . . .13g
Sugars	. . . . .0g
Fat	. . . . .28g
Saturates	. . . . .14g

INGREDIENTS

generous ½ cup all-purpose flour

½ tsp paprika

salt and pepper

6 tbsp butter, diced

generous ¾ cup water

3 eggs, lightly beaten

3 oz/85 g Swiss cheese, grated

corn oil, for deep-frying

½ cup freshly grated
Parmesan cheese

1 Sift the flour, paprika and ½ teaspoon salt together onto a sheet of waxed paper or parchment paper. Place the butter in a large, heavy-bottom pan, pour in the water, and heat gently. The moment the butter has melted and the liquid starts to boil, tip in the flour mixture and beat vigorously with a wooden spoon until the dough comes away from the side of the pan.

2 Remove the pan from the heat and let cool for 5 minutes. Gradually beat in the eggs to give a stiff, dropping consistency—you may not need all of them. Stir in the Swiss cheese.

3 Heat the corn oil to 350–375°F/ 180–190°C, or until a cube of bread browns in 30 seconds. Shape balls of choux dough between 2 teaspoons and drop them into the oil. Cook for 3–4 minutes, or until golden brown. Remove with a slotted spoon, drain on paper towels and keep warm until all the aigrettes are cooked. Pile onto a warmed serving dish, sprinkle with grated Parmesan cheese, and serve immediately.

cook's tip

When deep-frying, either use a deep-fryer or a large, deep, heavy bottom pan. Do not fill the deep-fryer more than half full with oil and the pan more than a third full.

pantry tuna

cook: 25 mins　　　　**prep: 5 mins**　　　　**serves 4**

NUTRITIONAL INFORMATION

Calories 458

Protein 23g

Carbohydrate 38g

Sugars 12g

Fat 25g

Saturates 11g

variation

Substitute canned mackerel for tuna
and if you prefer flavored potato
chips, like cheese and onion, use
these instead of plain.

*All the flavor of a fish pie with none of the hard work, this dish
is perfect for those days when you don't feel much like shopping
or cooking. Serve with crusty bread for a more substantial meal.*

INGREDIENTS

2 tbsp butter, plus
extra for greasing
scant ¼ cup all-purpose flour
1¼ cups milk
2 oz/55 g Cheddar cheese, grated
7 oz/200 g canned tuna in oil

11½ oz/325 g canned
corn, drained
salt and pepper
2 tomatoes, thinly sliced
2½ oz/70 g plain potato chips

cook's tip

You can cook this dish in the
microwave. Place the mixture
in a bowl, cover, and cook on
Medium for 5 minutes, or until
hot, stirring halfway through.
Transfer to a serving plate, add
the potato chips and serve.

1 Preheat the oven to
350°F/180°C. Melt the
butter in a large, heavy-
bottom pan. Sprinkle in the
flour and cook, stirring
constantly, for 1 minute.
Remove the pan from the heat
and gradually whisk in the
milk. Return to the heat, bring
to a boil, and cook, whisking
constantly, for 2 minutes.

2 Remove the pan from
the heat and stir in the
grated cheese. Flake the tuna
and add it to the mixture with
the oil from the can. Stir in the
corn and season to taste with
salt and pepper.

3 Lightly grease a large
ovenproof dish. Line the
dish with the tomato slices,
then spoon in the tuna
mixture. Crumble the potato
chips over the top and bake in
the preheated oven for
20 minutes. Serve.

exotic mushroom omelets

Eggs are a great stand-by when time is short, but they don't have to be boring. An omelet with a creamy mushroom filling, perhaps served with a green salad, is a dish fit for a king.

INGREDIENTS

2 tbsp butter

6 eggs, lightly beaten

salt and pepper

EXOTIC MUSHROOM FILLING

1 oz/25 g butter

5½ oz/150 g exotic mushrooms, sliced

2 tbsp sour cream

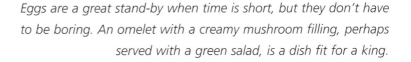

NUTRITIONAL INFORMATION	
Calories	.457
Protein	.21g
Carbohydrate	.2g
Sugars	.0g
Fat	.41g
Saturates	.21g

cook's tip

Use whatever mushrooms are available, such as morels, chanterelles, and portobello mushrooms. To clean, rinse morels and chanterelles and shake dry. Wipe portobello mushrooms with a damp cloth.

1 To make the exotic mushroom filling, heat the butter in a large, heavy-bottom skillet. Add the mushrooms and cook over low heat, stirring occasionally, for 5 minutes. Stir in the sour cream and season to taste with salt and pepper. Keep warm.

2 To make the omelets, melt half the butter in an omelet pan or small skillet over medium–high heat. Season the eggs to taste with salt and pepper, add half to the omelet pan and stir with a fork. As the egg sets, draw it toward the center and tilt the omelet pan so that the uncooked egg runs underneath. Cook until the underside of the omelet is golden and set, but the top is still moist.

3 Remove the omelet pan from the heat. Spoon half the mushroom mixture along a line just to one side of the center of the omelet. Flip the other side over and slide the omelet onto a plate. Keep warm. Melt the remaining butter and cook a second omelet in the same way. Serve immediately.

omelets with fines herbes

⏲ **cook: 4 mins**   ◔ **prep: 10 mins**   **serves 2**

This subtly flavored omelet would go well with a tomato salad and Vinaigrette dressing (see page 13) or mixed salad greens for a light, summery lunch.

NUTRITIONAL INFORMATION	
Calories	.320
Protein	.20g
Carbohydrate	.1g
Sugars	.0g
Fat	.27g
Saturates	.11g

INGREDIENTS

6 eggs

4 tbsp chopped fresh parsley

4 tbsp chopped fresh tarragon

4 tbsp chopped fresh chervil

2 tbsp chopped fresh chives

salt and pepper

1 oz/25 g butter

mixed salad greens, to serve

cook's tip

French fines herbes is a mix of four fresh aromatic herbs—tarragon, chives, parsley, and chervil. However, if you cannot find some of these herbs, then use marjoram, oregano, or dill instead.

1 Beat the eggs with the parsley, tarragon, chervil, and chives. Season to taste with salt and pepper.

2 Melt half the butter in an omelet pan or small, heavy-bottom skillet. Add half the egg mixture and stir with a fork. As the egg sets, draw it toward the center and tilt the omelet pan so that the uncooked egg runs underneath. Cook until the underside of the omelet is golden and set, but the top is still moist.

3 Remove the omelet pan from the heat and slide the omelet onto a plate, flipping the pan gently so that the omelet folds. Keep warm. Melt the remaining butter and cook a second omelet in the same way. Serve immediately with mixed salad greens.

eggs benedict

serves 4   **prep: 5 mins** ⏲   **cook: 25 mins** ⏲

This is really just a sophisticated version of the classic combination of ham and eggs and is just as satisfying.

INGREDIENTS

2 tbsp butter

4 slices ham

2 English muffins, split in half

4 eggs

fresh flatleaf parsley leaves, to garnish

HOLLANDAISE SAUCE

3 egg yolks

1–2 tbsp lemon juice

pinch of cayenne pepper

salt and pepper

8 oz/225 g unsalted butter, diced

NUTRITIONAL INFORMATION

Calories 711

Protein 18g

Carbohydrate 18g

Sugars 1g

Fat 64g

Saturates 37g

variation

For a cheat's version of Hollandaise sauce, heat ⅔ cup heavy cream and ⅔ cup mayonnaise, stirring constantly. Do not boil. Season.

cook's tip

When making Hollandaise sauce, if it becomes too thick, then slacken it with a little hot water. When the sauce is set over a pan of water, never let the water go above simmering point.

1 Preheat the broiler to medium. To make the Hollandaise sauce, whisk the egg yolks with 1 tablespoon of the lemon juice, the cayenne pepper, and salt and pepper to taste in a large, heavy-bottom pan. Add the butter and heat gently, whisking constantly, until the butter has melted and blended into the egg yolk. Remove the pan from the heat

and whisk until thick and creamy. Taste and add more lemon juice and seasoning, if necessary. Pour the sauce into a heatproof bowl and set over a pan of barely simmering water to keep warm.

2 Melt the butter in a skillet over low heat. Add the ham and cook, turning occasionally, for

5 minutes, or until heated through. Toast the English muffins under the preheated hot broiler at the same time.

3 Meanwhile, bring a small pan of water to a boil. Break an egg into a cup, stir the water to make a "whirlpool" and slide in the egg. Poach for 3–4 minutes, or until the white is set, but the

yolk is soft. Remove and drain. Poach the remaining eggs in the same way.

4 Place an English muffin half, cut-side up, on each of 4 warmed plates. Top each with a slice of ham and an egg. Stir the Hollandaise sauce and spoon it over the eggs. Serve, garnished with parsley leaves.

stuffed tomatoes

serves 4   **prep: 10 mins** ⏱   **cook: 20 mins** ⏱

Tomatoes and anchovies taste wonderful together and make a delicious, light meal. Serve hot or warm in the Mediterranean style.

INGREDIENTS

4 large tomatoes

8 canned anchovy fillets, drained and finely chopped

½ cup fresh white bread crumbs

1 garlic clove, finely chopped

1 tbsp olive oil

1 egg, lightly beaten

salt and pepper

crisp green salad, to serve

NUTRITIONAL INFORMATION

Calories	100
Protein	5g
Carbohydrate	8g
Sugars	5g
Fat	6g
Saturates	1g

cook's tip

Beefsteak tomatoes are ideal for filling as they are large and have a wonderful flavor. They should be ripe, but firm, to ensure that they hold their shape when stuffed and baked.

1 Preheat the oven to 375°F/190°C. Using a sharp knife, slice the tops from the tomatoes and set aside. Scoop out the flesh with a teaspoon and set aside. Stand the tomato shells upside down on paper towels to drain.

2 Mix the anchovies, bread crumbs, garlic, olive oil, and enough of the egg to bind the mixture together in a small bowl. Season to taste with salt and pepper.

3 Spoon the filling into the tomato shells and replace the tops. Arrange the tomatoes in a large ovenproof dish and bake in the preheated oven for 20 minutes. Transfer to a large serving plate and serve hot or warm with a crisp green salad.

fried green tomatoes

⏲ **cook: 10 mins**   ⏱ **prep: 5 mins**   **serves 4**

This crisp, golden snack is ready in minutes and undoubtedly deserves an Oscar for its performance.

NUTRITIONAL INFORMATION	
Calories	.255
Protein	.6g
Carbohydrate	.33g
Sugars	.5g
Fat	.11g
Saturates	.2g

INGREDIENTS

¾ cup coarse cornmeal

½ tsp garlic salt

1 tsp dried marjoram

2 tbsp all-purpose flour

salt and pepper

1 egg

4 large green or slightly underripe tomatoes, thickly sliced

corn oil, for deep-frying

cook's tip

Cornmeal is ground corn, and is also known as polenta. It is very popular in Italy and is available in several grades, from coarse to fine. Cornmeal is available in supermarkets and health food stores.

1 Place the cornmeal on a flat plate and stir in the garlic salt and marjoram. Place the flour on a second plate and season to taste with salt and pepper. Lightly beat the egg in a shallow bowl.

2 Dip the tomato slices first into the flour, then into the beaten egg and, finally, into the cornmeal to coat, then gently shake off any excess.

3 Pour the oil into a skillet to a depth of 1 inch/ 2.5 cm and heat. Add the coated tomato slices, in batches, and cook, turning once, until golden and crisp. Keep warm while you cook the remaining slices. Transfer to a large serving plate and serve immediately.

indonesian corn balls

serves 4   prep: 10 mins   cook: 10–15 mins

These spicy little vegetable balls can be served hot or cold as a delicious snack or as one of several dishes to make up a complete Indonesian meal.

INGREDIENTS

¾ cup unsalted peanuts

11½ oz/325 g canned corn, drained

1 onion, finely chopped

¾ cup all-purpose flour

1 tsp ground coriander

½ tsp sambal ulek or chili sauce

salt

1–2 tbsp warm water (optional)

peanut oil, for deep-frying

NUTRITIONAL INFORMATION	
Calories	.440
Protein	.13g
Carbohydrate	.49g
Sugars	.12g
Fat	.23g
Saturates	.4g

cook's tip

Sambal ulek is a fiery hot chili sauce available from Asian food stores and supermarkets. If you cannot find it, then use chili sauce instead.

1 Place the peanuts in a food processor and process briefly until coarsely ground. Alternatively, grind them in a mortar with a pestle. Transfer to a bowl and stir in the corn, onion, flour, coriander, and sambal ulek. Season to taste with salt. Knead to a dough, adding a little warm water, if necessary, to make the dough workable.

2 Heat the oil in a deep-fryer or large, heavy-bottom pan. Using your hands, form tablespoonfuls of the dough into balls, then drop the corn balls into the hot oil, in batches, and cook until golden and crisp.

3 Remove the corn balls with a slotted spoon, drain on paper towels and keep warm while you cook the remaining batches. Serve immediately or let cool first.

peanut fritters

cook: 10 mins   prep: 5 mins   serves 4

Popular with children and adults, these fritters are perfect for parties because they can be made in advance, stored in an airtight container, then reheated for 10 minutes in a medium–hot oven.

NUTRITIONAL INFORMATION

Calories 212

Protein 5g

Carbohydrate 15g

Sugars 3g

Fat 15g

Saturates 3g

INGREDIENTS

generous ⅜ cup rice flour

½ tsp baking powder

1 garlic clove, finely chopped

½ tsp ground turmeric

½ tsp ground coriander

⅛ tsp ground cumin

scant ½ cup unsalted peanuts, lightly crushed

½–⅔ cup coconut milk

salt

peanut oil, for cooking

cook's tip

Coconut milk is not the same as the liquid found in the fresh nut. It is available in cans from supermarkets and specialist Asian food stores.

1 Place the rice flour, baking powder, garlic, turmeric, coriander, cumin, and crushed peanuts together in a bowl and mix well. Gradually stir enough coconut milk into the mixture to make a smooth, thin batter. Season to taste with salt.

2 Pour the peanut oil into a heavy-bottom skillet to the depth of ½ inch/ 1 cm and heat.

3 Add spoonfuls of the batter to the skillet, spacing them well apart, and cook until the tops have just set and the undersides are golden. Turn and cook for 1 minute, or until the second side is golden. Remove with a spatula, drain on paper towels, and keep warm while you cook the remaining fritters.

meat & poultry

Fast food has become a synonym for unhealthy, unappealing, rather boring, and fairly tasteless meals, but the recipes featured here prove that this simply isn't true. They also show that you don't have to spend hours slaving over a hot stove to produce flavorsome, nourishing, and imaginative dishes, whether for family meals or entertaining friends, weekend lunches, or special occasions. Try Virginian Pork Chops (see page 129), served with peaches and a peppercorn sauce, or traditional Toad in the Hole with Onion Gravy (see page 144) for a midweek family supper; serve York Ham & Asparagus Rolls (see page 137) or Tarragon Chicken (see page 161) for an alfresco summer lunch; or impress at a dinner party with Tournedos Rossini (see page 125) or Butterflied Squab Chickens (see page 168).

Even the most inexperienced or unenthusiastic cooks can have an international repertoire of fabulous dishes at their fingertips, from Beef Stroganoff (see page 122) to Chicken Teriyaki (see page 157). Recipes feature beef, pork, lamb, turkey, and chicken—not to mention ham and sausages—and are broiled, braised, stir-fried, and oven-cooked. From spicy and aromatic to rich and creamy, there is a dish to suit all tastes and occasions—and most take no more than 30 minutes from kitchen to table.

beef stroganoff

serves 4   **prep: 5 mins**   **cook: 12–15 mins**

Tender strips of steak are cooked in a creamy mushroom sauce to make a special meal in minutes.

INGREDIENTS

generous ¼ cup all-purpose flour

1 tsp paprika

salt and pepper

1 lb 9 oz/700 g rump steak, very thinly sliced into strips

2 oz/55 g butter

1 onion, finely chopped

1 garlic clove, finely chopped

8 oz/225 g white mushrooms

1 tbsp lemon juice

2 tbsp dry red wine

2 tbsp tomato paste

1½ cups sour cream

2 tbsp chopped fresh chives, to garnish

NUTRITIONAL INFORMATION

Calories	.570
Protein	.44g
Carbohydrate	.16g
Sugars	.7g
Fat	.36g
Saturates	.21g

cook's tip

If you have time, wrap the steak tightly in plastic wrap and place in the freezer for 30 minutes. This will make it easier to slice wafer-thin.

1 Place the flour and paprika in a plastic bag and season with salt and pepper. Shake to mix, then add a few steak strips at a time and shake to coat.

2 Melt the butter in a large, heavy-bottom skillet. Add the onion and garlic and cook over low heat, stirring occasionally, for 5 minutes, or until softened. Increase the heat to high, add the steak strips and cook, stirring constantly, until browned all over. Stir in the mushrooms, lemon juice, and wine, reduce the heat, and let simmer for 5 minutes.

3 Stir in the tomato paste and sour cream and adjust the seasoning, if necessary. Serve immediately, garnished with the chives.

beef kabobs

cook: 8 mins   **prep: 15 mins**   serves 4

This simple dish tastes wonderful and would make a delicious treat for any occasion. It would also be ideal for a barbecue party.

NUTRITIONAL INFORMATION

Calories	.335
Protein	.40g
Carbohydrate	.2g
Sugars	.2g
Fat	.19g
Saturates	.4g

INGREDIENTS

8 scallions

1 lb 9 oz/700 g rump steak,
cut into cubes

8 cherry tomatoes, halved

1 tbsp whole-grain mustard

1 tsp Worcestershire sauce

½ tsp balsamic vinegar

4 tbsp corn oil

salt and pepper

cook's tip

It is much quicker to use metal skewers for this dish because wooden ones need to be soaked in warm water for 30 minutes before using to prevent them burning under the broiler or on the barbecue.

1 Preheat the broiler to medium. Cut the scallions into 4–5-inch/ 10–13-cm lengths and halve lengthwise. Thread the steak cubes, scallion lengths, and cherry tomato halves alternately onto 4 metal skewers. Arrange them on a broiler rack.

2 Mix the mustard, Worcestershire sauce, and vinegar together in a small bowl. Whisk in the corn oil and season to taste with salt and pepper.

3 Brush the kabobs with the flavored oil and cook under the preheated broiler for 4 minutes. Turn over, brush with the flavored oil again and cook for 4 minutes. Transfer to a large serving plate and serve immediately.

tournedos rossini

cook: 25 mins   **prep: 5 mins**   **serves 4**

Also known as filet mignon, tournedos is said to have got its name when a waiter, shocked by the composer Rossini asking for steak with foie gras and truffles, served the dish behind the backs of other customers. This is a rather less expensive, although still luxurious, version of the dish.

INGREDIENTS

4 slices fine chicken liver pâté	2 tbsp all-purpose flour
4 tournedos or round fillet steaks, about 1-inch/2.5-cm thick	scant 2 cups Beef Stock (see page 13)
4 oz/115 g butter	½ cup Madeira
4 oz/115 g mushrooms, sliced	salt and pepper
1 shallot, chopped	4 slices white bread, crusts removed

variation

Replace the shallot with a small, finely chopped onion and use cremini mushrooms, which have a stronger flavor than white mushrooms.

cook's tip

If you have time and would like a really tender cut of meat, then before cooking, place the steak between 2 sheets of plastic wrap and, using a rolling pin or meat mallet, pound lightly.

1 Preheat the broiler to medium. Cut the pâté to fit the top of the steaks and set aside. Melt 2 tablespoons of the butter in a large skillet. Add the mushrooms and cook over low heat for 5 minutes, or until tender. Remove with a slotted spoon and set aside. Add the shallot to the skillet and cook, stirring occasionally for 3–4 minutes, or until

softened. Sprinkle in the flour and cook, stirring constantly, for 1 minute. Remove the skillet from the heat and gradually stir in the Beef Stock and Madeira.

2 Return the skillet to the heat and bring to a boil, stirring constantly. Season to taste with salt and pepper, then let simmer for 5 minutes.

3 Dot the steaks with 2 tablespoons of the remaining butter and season to taste with pepper. Cook under the preheated hot broiler for 4 minutes on each side, or according to taste. Meanwhile, melt the remaining butter in a separate large, heavy-bottom skillet, add the bread and cook until golden brown on both sides.

4 Remove the steaks from the broiler and keep warm. Place the pâté slices in the juices in the broiler pan and return to the broiler to heat through. To serve, place a croûte on each of 4 plates and top with the steak. Place a pâté slice on top of each steak. Pour the pan juices into the sauce, strain, stir in the mushrooms, then serve with the steaks.

steak in orange sauce

serves 4　　　　　　**prep: 5 mins** ⏲　　　　　　**cook: 6–8 mins** ⏲

This is a delightful dish for a special occasion. You can use fillet or sirloin steak, as both are very tender cuts.

INGREDIENTS

2 large oranges

2 tbsp butter

4 fillet steaks, about 6 oz/175 g each

salt and pepper

6 tbsp Beef Stock (see page 13)

1 tbsp balsamic vinegar

fresh flatleaf parsley leaves, to garnish

NUTRITIONAL INFORMATION

Calories 330

Protein 38g

Carbohydrate 9g

Sugars 9g

Fat 16g

Saturates 8g

variation

Substitute 1 tablespoon Cointreau for 1 tablespoon of the orange juice in Step 1, if you prefer.

cook's tip

Balsamic vinegar comes from Modena in Italy and is the oldest and finest vinegar in the world. It is best used in simple dishes and in salad dressings. Balsamic vinegar is available from most large supermarkets.

1 Using a zester, pare a few strips of orange zest from 1 orange and set aside for the garnish. Cut the oranges in half, then cut off 4 thin slices and set aside for the garnish. Squeeze the juice from the remaining halves.

2 Melt the butter in a heavy-bottom skillet. Add the steaks and cook over medium heat for 1–2 minutes on each side, or until browned and sealed. Remove the steaks from the skillet, season to taste with salt and pepper, set aside, and keep warm.

3 Pour the orange juice into the skillet and add the Beef Stock and vinegar. Let simmer over low heat for 2 minutes. Season the orange sauce to taste with salt and pepper and return the steaks to the skillet. Heat through gently for 2 minutes, or according to taste. Transfer to warmed serving plates and garnish with the orange slices, orange zest, and parsley leaves. Serve immediately.

virginian pork chops

cook: 22 mins **prep: 5 mins** **serves 4**

Succulent peaches balance the richness of pork, complementing chops superbly and creating a colorful dish.

INGREDIENTS

2 tbsp corn oil

4 pork chops, about 6 oz/175 g each

2 tbsp white wine

1 onion, chopped

14½ oz/415 g canned peach halves in natural juice, drained

1 tbsp pink or green peppercorns

⅔ cup Chicken Stock (see page 13)

2–3 tsp balsamic vinegar

salt and pepper

variation

Substitute canned apricots for the peaches or use fresh fruit. Blanch, peel, pit, and slice fresh peaches or nectarines; halve and pit apricots.

cook's tip

Pink peppercorns are not a true pepper, but a processed berry from a South American tree. Green peppercorns are a true pepper. Buy freeze-dried or dehydrated peppercorns, not those in brine or vinegar.

1 Heat half the corn oil in a large, heavy-bottom skillet. Add the chops and cook for 6 minutes on each side, or until browned and cooked through. Transfer to a plate, cover, and keep warm. Pour off any excess fat from the skillet and return to the heat. Add the wine and cook, for 2 minutes, stirring and scraping up any sediment from the bottom of the skillet. Pour the liquid over the meat, re-cover, and keep warm.

2 Wipe out the skillet with paper towels and heat the remaining corn oil. Add the onion and cook over low heat, stirring occasionally, for 5 minutes, or until softened. Meanwhile, slice the peach halves.

3 Add the peaches to the skillet and heat through for 1 minute. Stir in the peppercorns, pour in the Chicken Stock, and bring to simmering point. Return the chops and cooking juices to the skillet and season to taste with vinegar, salt and pepper. Transfer to warmed plates and serve immediately.

neapolitan pork steaks

serves 4   prep: 10 mins   cook: 25 mins

An Italian version of broiled pork steaks served with fresh vegetables, this dish is easy to make and delicious to eat.

INGREDIENTS

2 tbsp olive oil

1 large onion, sliced

1 garlic clove, chopped

14 oz/400 g canned tomatoes

2 tsp yeast extract

4 pork loin steaks, about
4½ oz/125 g each

scant ½ cup black olives, pitted

2 tbsp fresh basil, shredded

freshly grated Parmesan cheese,
to garnish

green vegetables, to serve

NUTRITIONAL INFORMATION

Calories	.353
Protein	.39g
Carbohydrate	.4g
Sugars	.3g
Fat	.20g
Saturates	.5g

cook's tip

Parmesan is a mature and exceptionally hard cheese produced in Italy. You only need to add a little as it has a very strong flavor.

1 Preheat the broiler to medium. Heat the oil in a large skillet. Add the onion and garlic and cook, stirring, for 3–4 minutes, or until just starting to soften.

2 Add the tomatoes and yeast extract to the skillet and let simmer for 5 minutes, or until the sauce starts to thicken.

3 Cook the pork steaks, under the preheated broiler, for 5 minutes on both sides, until the the meat is cooked through. Set the pork aside and keep warm.

4 Add the olives and shredded basil to the sauce in the skillet and stir quickly to combine.

5 Transfer the steaks to warmed serving plates. Top with the sauce, garnish with freshly grated Parmesan cheese, and serve immediately with green vegetables.

pork with fennel & juniper

cook: 15 mins

prep: 15 mins, plus 2 hrs marinating

serves 4

The addition of juniper and fennel to pork chops gives an unusual and delicate flavor to this dish.

NUTRITIONAL INFORMATION

Calories 277

Protein 32g

Carbohydrate 0.4g

Sugars 0.4g

Fat 16g

Saturates 5g

INGREDIENTS

½ fennel bulb

1 tbsp juniper berries

about 2 tbsp olive oil

finely grated rind and juice of 1 orange

4 pork chops, about 5½ oz/150 g each

TO SERVE

crisp salad

fresh bread

cook's tip

Juniper berries are commonly associated with gin, but they are often added to meat dishes in Italy for a delicate citrus flavor. They can be bought dried from health food stores and large supermarkets.

1 Finely chop the fennel bulb, discarding the green parts.

2 Grind the juniper berries in a mortar and pestle. Mix the crushed juniper berries with the fennel flesh, olive oil, and orange rind.

3 Using a sharp knife, score a few cuts all over each pork chop. Place the chops in a roasting pan or ovenproof dish. Spoon the fennel and juniper mixture over the top. Pour over the orange juice, cover and let marinate in the refrigerator for 2 hours.

4 Preheat the broiler to medium. Cook the pork chops under the preheated broiler for 10–15 minutes, depending on the thickness of the meat, or until the meat is tender and cooked through, turning occasionally.

5 Transfer the chops to serving plates and serve with a crisp, fresh salad and plenty of fresh bread to mop up the cooking juices.

pork stir-fry

serves 4   prep: 15 mins ⌛   cook: 12 mins ⏲

Stir-fries are always a popular choice for a midweek supper, as they introduce variety into the week's menus and are quick to cook.

INGREDIENTS

2 tbsp dark soy sauce

1 tbsp Chinese rice wine

1 tbsp Chinese rice vinegar

1 tbsp soft brown sugar

1 tsp Chinese five-spice powder

8 oz/225 g canned
pineapple rings in juice

1 tbsp cornstarch

1 tbsp peanut oil

4 scallions, chopped

1 garlic clove, finely chopped

1-inch/2.5-cm piece of fresh gingerroot,
finely chopped

12 oz/350 g pork loin, cut into
very thin strips

3 carrots, cut into thin sticks

6 oz/175 g baby corn

1 green bell pepper, seeded and
cut into thin sticks

¾ cup bean sprouts

4 oz/115 g snow peas

NUTRITIONAL INFORMATION	
Calories 274	
Protein 23g	
Carbohydrate 25g	
Sugars 16g	
Fat 10g	
Saturates 3g	

variation

Substitute the Chinese rice wine with the same amount of dry sherry and replace the snow peas with the same amount of sugar snap peas.

cook's tip

Chinese five-spice powder, which is different from the Indian blend, consists of Sichuan pepper, fennel, cloves, cinnamon, and star anise.

1 Mix the soy sauce, rice wine, rice vinegar, sugar, and five-spice powder together in a bowl. Drain the pineapple, reserving the juice in a measuring cup. Chop the pineapple and set aside until required. Stir the cornstarch into the pineapple juice until a smooth paste forms, then stir the paste into the soy sauce mixture and set aside.

2 Heat the peanut oil in a preheated wok or large, heavy-bottom skillet. Add the scallions, garlic, and ginger and stir-fry for 30 seconds. Add the pork strips and stir-fry for 3 minutes, or until browned all over.

3 Add the carrots, baby corn, and green bell pepper and stir-fry for

3 minutes. Add the bean sprouts and snow peas and stir-fry for 2 minutes. Add the pineapple and the soy sauce mixture and cook, stirring constantly, for an additional 2 minutes, or until slightly thickened. Transfer to warmed serving bowls and serve immediately.

pork in creamy mushroom sauce

⏲ **cook: 15 mins**   ⏱ **prep: 10 mins**   **serves 4**

The perfect choice for easy entertaining, as the dish looks and tastes fabulous, but is actually astonishingly simple to prepare.

INGREDIENTS

2 tbsp unsalted butter

1 lb 9 oz/700 g pork loin, cut into thin strips

salt and pepper

10 oz/280 g mixed exotic and cultivated mushrooms, halved, or quartered if large

6 tbsp dry white wine

1 cup sour cream

1 tbsp chopped fresh sage

variation

If exotic mushrooms are not available, use white mushrooms and add ¼ cup dried porcini, soaked in hot water for 20 minutes, then drained.

cook's tip

If possible, try to use fresh herbs as they have a much better flavor than dried. If they are not available, use freeze-dried herbs instead. These are found in most large supermarkets.

1 Melt the butter in a large, heavy-bottom skillet. Add the pork strips and cook over medium–low heat, stirring frequently, for 5 minutes, or until browned all over. Transfer to a plate with a slotted spoon, season to taste with salt and pepper, cover, and keep warm.

2 Add the mushrooms to the skillet and cook, stirring frequently, for 5–7 minutes, or until tender. Add the wine, bring to a boil, and cook until reduced. Add the sour cream and return to a boil.

3 Return the pork to the skillet, stir in the sage, and heat through for 1–2 minutes. Transfer to a warmed serving dish and serve immediately.

gammon in madeira sauce

serves 4　　　　**prep: 5 mins** ⏲　　　　**cook: 15 mins** ⏲

This is an easy version of an old-fashioned recipe that involves rather more time and effort. It is just as delicious. Serve with freshly cooked vegetables and potatoes for a tasty, nutritious supper.

INGREDIENTS

4 gammon steaks,
about 8 oz/225 g each

2 tbsp butter

2 cloves

1 mace blade

1 cup Madeira

2 tsp Meaux mustard

fresh flatleaf parsley sprigs,
to garnish

NUTRITIONAL INFORMATION

Calories	.493
Protein	.67g
Carbohydrate	.2g
Sugars	.2g
Fat	.18g
Saturates	.8g

1 Snip the edges of the gammon steaks with kitchen scissors to prevent them from curling up as they cook.

2 Melt the butter in a large, heavy-bottom skillet, then add the cloves and mace blade. Add the gammon, in batches if necessary, and cook for 3 minutes on each side. Transfer to a warmed dish, cover, and keep warm.

3 Add the Madeira to the skillet and bring to a boil, stirring and scraping up any sediment from the bottom of the skillet. Stir in the mustard and cook for 2 minutes, or until the sauce is thickened and glossy. Pour the sauce over the gammon, garnish with parsley sprigs, and serve immediately.

cook's tip

Mace is available in blades and ready ground. Try to buy blades, as the ground powder deteriorates rapidly. Store mace blades in a cool place in an airtight container.

york ham & asparagus rolls

⏱ **cook: 25 mins**   ⏲ **prep: 5 mins**   **serves 6**

You can't really go wrong with a mixture of lean ham, asparagus, and creamy cheese sauce. This dish makes a great main meal, but it can also be served as an appetizer for 8–10 people.

NUTRITIONAL INFORMATION

Calories	.464
Protein	.33g
Carbohydrate	.15g
Sugars	.7g
Fat	.31g
Saturates	.18g

INGREDIENTS

**1 lb 14 oz/850 g canned asparagus
spears, drained**

12 slices cooked York ham

CHEESE SAUCE

2 oz/55 g butter

⅜ cup all-purpose flour

2½ cups milk

1 tbsp Dijon mustard

5 oz/140 g Cheddar cheese, grated

5½ oz/150 g Swiss cheese, grated

pinch of freshly grated nutmeg

salt and pepper

cook's tip

York ham is one of the British specially cured hams that is still preserved by the old traditional methods. If unavailable, then use a high-quality country-style ham instead.

1 Preheat the oven to 350°F/180°C. To make the sauce, melt the butter in a large, heavy-bottom pan. Sprinkle in the flour and cook, stirring constantly, for 1 minute. Remove the pan from the heat and gradually whisk in the milk. Return the pan to the heat and bring to a boil, stirring constantly. Cook until smooth and thickened, then remove from the heat and stir in the mustard, Cheddar, and Swiss cheese. Season to taste with nutmeg, salt, and pepper.

2 Divide the asparagus between the slices of ham. Roll up the ham and place, seam-side down, in a large ovenproof dish. Pour the sauce over the ham rolls.

3 Bake in the preheated oven for 20 minutes. Serve immediately.

spanish chops

serves 4   **prep: 5 mins**   **cook: 25 mins**

Bell peppers, tomatoes, olives, and herbs add color and flavor to this simple dish of lamb chops.

INGREDIENTS

1 tbsp olive oil	14 oz/400 g canned chopped tomatoes
1 onion, sliced	2 tsp chopped fresh thyme
1 garlic clove, finely chopped	1 tsp chopped fresh rosemary
2 red bell peppers, seeded and sliced	2 tbsp black olives
8 lamb loin chops, trimmed of excess fat	salt and pepper

NUTRITIONAL INFORMATION

Calories	.465
Protein	.17g
Carbohydrate	.9g
Sugars	.8g
Fat	.40g
Saturates	.19g

variation

Substitute the red bell peppers with yellow or orange bell peppers and replace the onion with a red onion.

cook's tip

You can buy olives that have already been pitted from most supermarkets, although try not to buy those stored in brine as they may make the finished dish too salty.

1 Heat the olive oil in a large, heavy-bottom skillet. Add the onion, garlic, and red bell peppers and cook over low heat, stirring occasionally, for 5 minutes, or until softened.

2 Increase the heat to medium, add the lamb chops and cook for 1–2 minutes on each side, or until browned.

3 Add the chopped tomatoes, thyme, and rosemary, then cover and let simmer for 15 minutes, or until the lamb is tender. Stir in the olives, season to taste with salt and pepper, and serve immediately, straight from the skillet.

lamb with olives

serves 4　　　　　**prep: 15 mins** ☾　　　　　**cook: 1 hr 30 mins** ☼

This is a very simple dish, and the chile adds a bit of spiciness. It is quick to prepare and makes an ideal supper dish.

INGREDIENTS

2 lb 12 oz/1.25 kg boned leg of lamb

6 tbsp olive oil

2 garlic cloves, crushed

1 onion, sliced

1 small, fresh red chile, cored, seeded, and finely chopped

¾ cup dry white wine

1 cup pitted black olives

salt

fresh parsley sprigs, to garnish

crusty bread, to serve

NUTRITIONAL INFORMATION

Calories 577

Protein 62g

Carbohydrate 1g

Sugars 1g

Fat 33g

Saturates 10g

variation

You could garnish this dish with fresh cilantro instead of parsley. Serve with warm ciabatta or focaccia instead of plain bread, if you like.

1 Preheat the oven to 350°F/180°C. Using a sharp knife, cut the lamb into 1-inch/2.5-cm cubes.

2 Heat the oil in a skillet, add the garlic, onion, and chile and cook for 5 minutes. Add the meat and wine and cook for an additional 5 minutes.

3 Stir in the olives, then transfer the mixture to a casserole. Bake in the preheated oven for 1 hour 20 minutes, or until the meat is tender. Season with salt to taste, garnish with chopped fresh parsley, and serve.

lamb with bay & lemon

 cook: 35 mins   prep: 10 mins   serves 4

These lamb chops quickly become more elegant and sophisticated when the bone is removed to make small, tender noisettes.

NUTRITIONAL INFORMATION

Calories 268

Protein 24g

Carbohydrate 0.2g

Sugars 0.2g

Fat 16g

Saturates 7g

INGREDIENTS

4 lamb chops

1 tbsp olive oil

1 tbsp butter

⅔ cup white wine

⅔ cup lamb or Vegetable Stock (see page 13)

2 bay leaves

pared rind of 1 lemon

salt and pepper

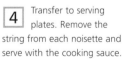

(see page 13)

cook's tip

Your local butcher will offer you good advice on how to prepare the lamb noisettes if you have not prepared them before.

1 Using a sharp knife, carefully remove the bone from each lamb chop, keeping the meat intact. Shape the meat into circles and secure with a length of string. Alternatively, ask your butcher to prepare the noisettes.

2 Place the oil and butter in a large skillet and heat until the mixture starts to froth. Add the noisettes to the skillet and cook for 2–3 minutes on each side, or until browned. Remove the skillet from the heat and drain off and discard the excess fat.

3 Return the skillet to the heat. Add the wine, stock, bay leaves, and lemon rind and cook for 20–25 minutes, or until the lamb is tender. Season the lamb noisettes and sauce with salt and pepper to taste.

4 Transfer to serving plates. Remove the string from each noisette and serve with the cooking sauce.

stir-fried lamb

⏲ **cook: 15 mins**   ⏱ **prep: 10 mins**   **serves 4**

Lamb is a less popular choice for stir-frying than beef or pork, yet it works very well, as this mint-flavored medley of neck fillet and crisp vegetables demonstrates.

INGREDIENTS

4 tbsp peanut oil	7½ cups fresh spinach leaves
1 lb 4 oz/550 g neck fillet of lamb, thinly sliced	2 tbsp lime juice
	3 tbsp oyster sauce
1 large onion, finely chopped	2 tbsp Thai fish sauce
2 garlic cloves, finely chopped	2 tsp superfine sugar
2 fresh red chiles, seeded and thinly sliced	5 tbsp chopped fresh mint
6 oz/175 g snow peas	salt and pepper

variation

Replace the lime juice with the same amount of lemon juice and if you don't like it too spicy, use just 1 fresh red chile.

cook's tip

Oyster sauce is a thick soy sauce, which is flavored with oyster juice. The flavor is very delicate and is ideal for dishes that need livening up. It is found in most supermarkets and Asian food stores.

1 Heat the peanut oil in a preheated wok or large, heavy-bottom skillet. Add the lamb and stir-fry over high heat for 2–3 minutes, or until browned all over. Remove with a slotted spoon and drain on paper towels.

2 Add the onion, garlic, and chiles to the wok and stir-fry for 3 minutes. Add the snow peas and stir-fry for 2 minutes, then stir in the spinach leaves and return the lamb to the wok.

3 Add the lime juice, oyster sauce, Thai fish sauce, and sugar, and cook, stirring constantly, for 4 minutes, or until the lamb is cooked through and tender. Stir in the chopped mint, season to taste with salt and pepper, and serve immediately.

toad in the hole with onion gravy

serves 4   **prep: 5 mins** ↺   **cook: 20 mins** ⏲

This traditional English dish was originally made with pieces of cooked meat and bacon, although nowadays pork sausages are usually used. As no amphibians of any kind have ever featured, its name remains somewhat obscure.

INGREDIENTS

8 pork sausages	**ONION GRAVY**
2 tbsp shortening or	**2 tbsp corn oil**
2 tbsp vegetable oil	**1 onion, chopped**
3 eggs	**1 tbsp all-purpose flour**
salt and pepper	**scant 1 cup Chicken Stock**
1¼ cups milk	**(see page 13)**
¾ cup all-purpose flour	**1 tsp red wine vinegar**
	salt and pepper

NUTRITIONAL INFORMATION

Calories	.780
Protein	.23g
Carbohydrate	.44g
Sugars	.8g
Fat	.58g
Saturates	.21g

variation

For extra-crisp batter, replace half the milk with water, and for extra flavor, stir in 1 teaspoon dried thyme.

cook's tip

Switch on the oven to preheat before you so much as wash your hands. It is essential that the oven and the muffin pan are very hot before you bake the batter.

1 Preheat the oven to 450°F/230°C. Using kitchen scissors, cut in between the sausages to separate them, spread them out on a baking sheet and partially cook in the preheated oven for 10 minutes, while you make the batter. Grease the cups of a muffin pan with the shortening, and place in the oven to heat up.

2 Using a balloon whisk, lightly beat the eggs with salt and pepper to taste in a small bowl, then add half the milk. Sift the flour into a large bowl, add the egg mixture, and stir until a smooth batter forms. Stir in the remaining milk. Remove the sausages and muffin pan from the oven and place 2 sausages in each cup. Pour in the batter and return to the oven for 10 minutes, or until the batter is puffed up and golden.

3 Meanwhile, make the onion gravy. Heat the oil in a large pan, add the onion and cook over low heat, stirring occasionally, for 5 minutes, or until softened. Sprinkle in the flour and cook, stirring, for 1 minute. Remove the pan from the heat and gradually stir in the Chicken Stock.

4 Return to the heat and bring to a boil, stirring constantly. Stir in the vinegar and season to taste with salt and pepper. Remove the toad in the hole from the oven and serve, handing the gravy separately.

fresh spaghetti & meatballs

serves 4 **prep: 45 mins** **cook: 1 hr 15 mins**

This well-loved Italian dish is famous across the world. Make the most of it by using high-quality steak for the meatballs.

INGREDIENTS

2¾ cups brown bread crumbs

⅔ cup milk

2 tbsp butter

generous ⅛ cup whole-wheat flour

scant 1 cup Beef Stock (see page 13)

14 oz/400 g canned chopped tomatoes

2 tbsp tomato paste

1 tsp sugar

1 tbsp finely chopped fresh tarragon

salt and pepper

1 large onion, chopped

2 cups ground steak

1 tsp paprika

4 tbsp olive oil

1 lb/450 g fresh spaghetti

fresh tarragon leaves, to garnish

NUTRITIONAL INFORMATION	
Calories	.665
Protein	.39g
Carbohydrate	.77g
Sugars	.9g
Fat	.24g
Saturates	.8g

variation

You can use peeled, chopped fresh tomatoes instead of canned tomatoes, but add an extra tablespoon of tomato paste to boost their flavor.

cook's tip

Fresh spaghetti cooks very quickly when placed straight into boiling water. Be careful not to overcook it, otherwise it will taste sticky and heavy.

1 Place the bread crumbs in a bowl, add the milk, and set aside to soak for about 30 minutes.

2 Preheat the oven to 350°F/180°C. Melt half of the butter in a pan. Add the flour and cook, stirring constantly, for 2 minutes. Gradually stir in the Beef Stock and cook, stirring, for an

additional 5 minutes. Add the tomatoes, tomato paste, sugar, and tarragon. Season well with salt and pepper and let simmer for 25 minutes.

3 Mix the onion, steak, and paprika into the bread crumbs and season to taste with salt and pepper. Shape the mixture into 14 meatballs.

4 Heat the oil and remaining butter in a skillet, add the meatballs, and cook, turning, until browned. Place in a deep casserole, pour over the tomato sauce, cover, and bake in the preheated oven for 25 minutes.

5 Bring a large pan of lightly salted water to a boil. Add the spaghetti,

return to a boil, and cook for 2–3 minutes, or until tender but still firm to the bite.

6 Meanwhile, remove the meatballs from the oven. Let cool for 3 minutes. Serve the meatballs and sauce on top of the spaghetti, garnished with tarragon leaves.

neapolitan veal cutlets

serves 4   **prep: 20 mins** ⟳   **cook: 45 mins** ⟳

*The delicious combination of apple, onion, and mushrooms
perfectly complements the delicate flavor of veal.*

INGREDIENTS

7 oz/200 g butter

4 veal cutlets, about 9 oz/250 g
each, trimmed

1 large onion, sliced

2 apples, peeled, cored, and sliced

6 oz/175 g white mushrooms

1 tbsp chopped fresh tarragon

8 black peppercorns

1 tbsp sesame seeds

salt and pepper

14 oz/400 g dried marille

generous ⅓ cup extra virgin olive oil

¾ cup mascarpone cheese

2 large beefsteak tomatoes, cut in half

leaves of 1 fresh basil sprig, plus

a few leaves, to garnish

NUTRITIONAL INFORMATION	
Calories 1071	
Protein 74g	
Carbohydrate 66g	
Sugars 13g	
Fat 59g	
Saturates 16g	

variation

You can also use tagliatelle or
tagliarini for this dish. If you like,
replace the mascarpone cheese
with sour cream.

cook's tip

Use eating apples such as
Baldwin or Braeburn apples for
this dish. You can place the
sliced apples in cold water
with a little lemon juice added
to prevent them going brown
before cooking.

 1 Preheat the oven
to 300°F/150°C. Place
2 ovenproof dishes in the oven
to warm. Melt 2 oz/55 g of
the butter in a skillet. Add the
veal and cook over low heat
for 5 minutes on each side.
Transfer to a warmed
ovenproof dish and place in
the oven to keep warm. Add
the onion and apples to the
skillet and cook until lightly

browned. Transfer to the other
ovenproof dish, place the veal
on top, and keep warm.

2 Melt the remaining
butter in the skillet.
Add the mushrooms,
tarragon, and peppercorns
and cook gently over low
heat for 3 minutes. Sprinkle
over the sesame seeds.

3 Preheat the broiler to
medium. Bring a pan of
salted water to a boil. Add the
pasta and 1 tablespoon of the
oil. Cook for 8–10 minutes,
until tender but firm to the bite.
Meanwhile, broil the tomatoes
and basil for 2–3 minutes.

4 Drain the pasta and
transfer to a serving
plate. Spoon the mascarpone

cheese on top and sprinkle
over the remaining olive oil.
Place the onions, apples, and
veal cutlets on top of the
pasta. Spoon the mushrooms,
peppercorns, and pan juices
onto the cutlets, place the
tomatoes and basil leaves
round the edge, and bake in
the oven for 5 minutes. Season
to taste, garnish with basil
leaves, and serve immediately.

veal italienne

serves 4   **prep: 25 mins** ☕   **cook: 1 hr 20 mins** ⏲

This dish is really superb if made with tender veal. However, if veal is unavailable, use pork or turkey scallops instead.

INGREDIENTS

2 oz/55 g butter	⅔ cup red wine
1 tbsp olive oil	1¼ cups Chicken Stock (see page 13)
1 lb 8 oz/675 g potatoes, cubed	8 ripe tomatoes, peeled, seeded,
4 veal scallops, about 6 oz/175 g each	and diced
1 onion, cut into 8 wedges	1 tbsp pitted black olives, halved
2 garlic cloves, crushed	2 tbsp chopped fresh basil, plus a few
2 tbsp all-purpose flour	leaves, to garnish
2 tbsp tomato paste	salt and pepper

NUTRITIONAL INFORMATION

Calories	.592
Protein	.44g
Carbohydrate	.48g
Sugars	.5g
Fat	.23g
Saturates	.9g

variation

To save time, you can substitute 14 oz/400 g canned chopped tomatoes for the fresh tomatoes.

cook's tip

For a quicker cooking time and really tender meat, pound the veal with a meat mallet to flatten it slightly before you start cooking.

1 Preheat the oven to 350°F/180°C. Heat the butter and oil in a large skillet. Add the potato cubes and cook for 5–7 minutes, stirring frequently, until starting to brown. Remove the potatoes from the skillet with a slotted spoon and set aside.

2 Place the veal in the skillet and cook for 2–3 minutes on each side, until sealed. Remove from the skillet and set aside.

3 Add the onion and garlic to the skillet and cook for 2–3 minutes. Add the flour and tomato paste and

cook for 1 minute, stirring. Gradually blend in the red wine and Stock, stirring to make a smooth sauce.

4 Return the potatoes and veal to the skillet. Stir in the tomatoes, olives, and chopped basil and season to taste with salt and pepper.

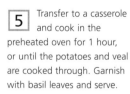

5 Transfer to a casserole and cook in the preheated oven for 1 hour, or until the potatoes and veal are cooked through. Garnish with basil leaves and serve.

veal in a rose petal sauce

serves 4　　　　　prep: 10 mins ☍　　　　　cook: 35 mins ⏲

This truly spectacular dish is equally delicious whether you use veal or pork fillet. Make sure the roses are free of blemishes and pesticides.

INGREDIENTS

1 lb/450 g dried fettuccine

generous ⅓ cup olive oil

1 tsp chopped fresh oregano

1 tsp chopped fresh marjoram

6 oz/175 g butter

1 lb/450 g veal fillet, thinly sliced

⅔ cup rose petal vinegar
(see Cook's Tip)

⅔ cup fish stock

¼ cup grapefruit juice

¼ cup heavy cream

salt

TO GARNISH

12 pink grapefruit segments

12 pink peppercorns

rose petals, washed

fresh herb leaves

NUTRITIONAL INFORMATION

Calories	.810
Protein	.31g
Carbohydrate	.49g
Sugars	.2g
Fat	.56g
Saturates	.28g

variation

This dish also tastes good served with fresh tagliatelle or tagliarini, which can be cooked while the veal is cooking in Step 2.

cook's tip

To make the rose petal vinegar, infuse the petals of 8 pesticide-free roses in ⅔ cup white wine vinegar for 48 hours. Make this well in advance to reduce the preparation time.

1 Bring a large pan of lightly salted water to a boil. Add the fettuccine and 1 tablespoon of the oil and cook for 8–10 minutes, or until tender but still firm to the bite. Drain and transfer to a warmed serving dish, sprinkle over 2 tablespoons of the olive oil, the oregano, and the marjoram. Keep warm.

2 Heat 2 oz/55 g of the butter with the remaining oil in a skillet. Add the veal and cook over low heat for 6 minutes. Remove the veal from the skillet and place on top of the pasta.

3 Add the vinegar and fish stock to the skillet and bring to a boil. Boil vigorously until reduced by two thirds. Add the grapefruit juice and cream and let simmer over low heat for 4 minutes. Dice the remaining butter and add to the skillet, one piece at a time, whisking constantly until completely incorporated.

4 Pour the sauce round the veal, then garnish with the pink grapefruit segments, pink peppercorns, and rose petals. Scatter over your favorite herb leaves and serve.

turkey breasts with orange sauce

⏱ **cook: 10 mins**   🕐 **prep: 10 mins**   **serves 4**

This is a fragrant, summery dish that needs nothing more than a crisp salad and fresh rolls to make a satisfying supper.

INGREDIENTS

4 turkey breast steaks,
about 5 oz/140 g each

salt and pepper

2 oz/55 g butter

2 tbsp olive oil

6 tbsp Chicken Stock (see page 13)

3–4 tbsp orange juice

1 tbsp chopped fresh chervil

TO GARNISH

orange slices

fresh chervil sprigs

variation

To make a lemon sauce, simply substitute lemon juice for the orange juice, lemon slices for the orange slices, and lemon balm for the chervil.

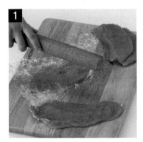

cook's tip

Blood oranges are a good choice for this dish, as they are very juicy and have a sharp edge to their flavor. If you cannot find blood oranges, then use ordinary ones instead.

1 Place each turkey breast steak in turn between 2 sheets of plastic wrap and beat with the side of a rolling pin or the flat surface of a meat mallet until about ¼ inch/5 mm thick. Season to taste with salt and pepper.

2 Melt half the butter with the oil in a large, grill pan. Add two of the turkey steaks and cook over high heat, turning once, for 3–4 minutes, or until lightly browned on both sides. Remove from the grill pan, add the remaining turkey steaks, 1 at a time, and cook in the same way. Keep warm.

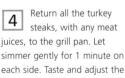

3 Pour the Chicken Stock into the grill pan and bring to a boil, stirring and scraping up any sediment from the bottom of the pan. Add 3 tablespoons of the orange juice, the remaining butter, and the chervil, then reduce the heat to a simmer.

4 Return all the turkey steaks, with any meat juices, to the grill pan. Let simmer gently for 1 minute on each side. Taste and adjust the seasoning, adding more orange juice if necessary. Serve immediately, garnished with orange slices and chervil sprigs.

chicken cordon bleu

serves 4 **prep: 5 mins** ☾ **cook: 25 mins** 🕛

Once extremely trendy and popular, this dish has rather gone out of fashion, which is a shame because it has a lovely flavor and texture, as well as being simplicity itself to prepare.

INGREDIENTS

4 skinless, boneless chicken breasts, about 5 oz/140 g each

4 slices cooked ham

4 tbsp grated Swiss cheese

salt and pepper

2 tbsp olive oil

4 oz/115 g white mushrooms, sliced

4 tbsp dry white wine

NUTRITIONAL INFORMATION

Calories	.300
Protein	.40g
Carbohydrate	.1g
Sugars	.1g
Fat	.15g
Saturates	.5g

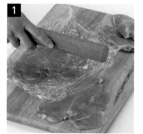

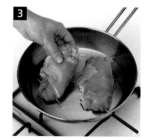

variation

Substitute 4 oz/115 g thinly sliced ricotta cheese for the Swiss cheese and replace the white mushrooms with cremini mushrooms.

1 Place each chicken breast in turn between 2 sheets of plastic wrap and beat with the side of a rolling pin or the flat surface of a meat mallet until about ¼ inch/5 mm thick.

2 Lay a slice of ham on each chicken breast and sprinkle 1 tablespoon of the Swiss cheese over half of each slice. Season to taste with salt and pepper. Fold the chicken over and secure with wooden toothpicks.

3 Heat the olive oil in a large, heavy-bottom skillet. Add the chicken and cook over high heat for 2–3 minutes on each side, or until golden brown. Remove from the skillet and keep warm. Add the mushrooms to the skillet and cook, stirring, for 2–3 minutes, or until browned, then return the chicken to the skillet and pour in the wine.

4 Reduce the heat and let simmer for 15 minutes, or until the chicken is tender and cooked through. Remove the toothpicks and serve the chicken with the mushrooms.

chicken teriyaki

cook: 15 mins   **prep: 15 mins**   **serves 4**

This Japanese-style stir-fry is full of flavor, although it is marinated for only a brief time. For an authentic flavor, use tamari—Japanese soy sauce—if available.

NUTRITIONAL INFORMATION	
Calories	.348
Protein	.29g
Carbohydrate	.51g
Sugars	.1g
Fat	.4g
Saturates	.1g

INGREDIENTS

1 lb/450 g skinless, boneless chicken breasts, thinly sliced into strips

2 tbsp tamari or dark soy sauce

1 tbsp Chinese rice wine

1 tbsp dry sherry

1 tsp sugar

grated rind of 1 orange

generous 1 cup long-grain rice

scant 2½ cups water

pinch of salt

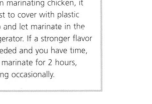

cook's tip

When marinating chicken, it is best to cover with plastic wrap and let marinate in the refrigerator. If a stronger flavor is needed and you have time, let it marinate for 2 hours, turning occasionally.

1 Place the chicken strips in a large, shallow dish. Mix the tamari, rice wine, sherry, sugar, and orange rind together in a measuring cup, stirring until the sugar has dissolved. Pour the marinade over the chicken, stir to coat, cover, and let marinate for 15 minutes.

2 Meanwhile, place the rice in a large, heavy-bottom pan. Pour in the water, add the salt, and bring to a boil. Stir once, reduce the heat, cover tightly, and let simmer very gently for 10 minutes. Remove the pan from the heat, but do not remove the lid.

3 Heat a wok or large, heavy-bottom skillet. Add the chicken and the marinade and cook, stirring constantly, for 5 minutes, or until the chicken is cooked through and tender. Remove the lid from the rice and fork through the grains to fluff up, then serve immediately with the chicken.

chinese chicken

serves 4   **prep: 10 mins** ⟳   **cook: 4 mins** ⟳

As in all Chinese dishes, the matching and contrasting flavors, colors, and textures in this recipe produce a harmonious—and utterly delicious—result.

INGREDIENTS

10 oz/280 g skinless, boneless chicken breasts, very thinly sliced

¼ tsp cornstarch

1¼ tsp water

1 small egg white, lightly beaten

salt

4 tbsp peanut oil

2 scallions, cut into short lengths

4 oz/115 g green beans, halved

8 shiitake mushrooms, halved if large

4 oz/115 g canned bamboo shoots, drained and rinsed

1 tsp finely chopped fresh gingerroot

1 tbsp dark soy sauce

1 tbsp Chinese rice wine or dry sherry

1 tsp light brown sugar

dash of sesame oil

NUTRITIONAL INFORMATION	
Calories	.214
Protein	.18g
Carbohydrate	.4g
Sugars	.2g
Fat	.14g
Saturates	.3g

variation

Substitute the shiitake mushrooms with exotic mushrooms, such as chanterelles, if you like.

cook's tip

Sesame oil is widely used in Chinese and Asian dishes. It is usually used as a flavoring at the end of cooking as it burns very easily.

1 Cut the chicken slices into small pieces and place in a bowl. Mix the cornstarch and water together until a smooth paste forms and add to the chicken with the egg white and a pinch of salt. Stir well to coat.

2 Heat the peanut oil in a preheated wok or large, heavy-bottom skillet. Add the chicken and stir-fry over medium heat for 45 seconds, or until browned. Remove from the wok with a slotted spoon.

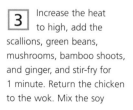

3 Increase the heat to high, add the scallions, green beans, mushrooms, bamboo shoots, and ginger, and stir-fry for 1 minute. Return the chicken to the wok. Mix the soy sauce and rice wine together in a small measuring cup and add to the wok with the sugar and a pinch of salt. Cook, stirring constantly, for an additional 1 minute. Sprinkle with a dash of sesame oil and serve immediately.

honey-glazed chicken

serves 4   **prep: 5 mins** ⏱   **cook: 20 mins** ⏱

This honey glaze can be brushed on any cuts of chicken—thighs are used here—before broiling or cooking on the barbecue.

INGREDIENTS

8 skinless chicken thighs

salt

GLAZE

scant 1¼ cups medium sherry

1 tbsp cornstarch

3 tbsp honey

3 tbsp red wine vinegar

1 tbsp dark soy sauce

3 garlic cloves, finely chopped

NUTRITIONAL INFORMATION

Calories	.300
Protein	.23g
Carbohydrate	.24g
Sugars	.16g
Fat	.6g
Saturates	.2g

cook's tip

If the juices run clear and not pink when the thickest part of the chicken is pierced with a skewer or the tip of a knife, it is cooked through.

1 Preheat the broiler to medium. To make the glaze, pour 1 cup of the sherry into a small pan and bring to a boil. Continue to boil for 6 minutes, or until reduced by half. Meanwhile, mix the remaining sherry and cornstarch together in a bowl until a smooth paste forms.

2 Remove the sherry from the heat and whisk in the honey, vinegar, soy sauce, and garlic. Return the pan to the heat and whisk in the cornstarch paste. Let simmer, whisking constantly, for 1 minute, then remove from the heat and let cool slightly.

3 Season the chicken with salt and place them on a broiler rack. Brush generously with the glaze and cook under the preheated broiler for 7 minutes.

4 Turn the chicken over, brush generously with the glaze and broil for an additional 3–4 minutes, or until the chicken is completely cooked through and tender. Transfer to warmed serving plates and serve immediately.

tarragon chicken

cook: 20 mins   **prep: 5 mins**   **serves 4**

This is a classic French recipe and it is such a stylish, yet understated dish that it would be a good choice for an informal dinner party.

NUTRITIONAL INFORMATION

Calories	.420
Protein	.39g
Carbohydrate	.2g
Sugars	.1g
Fat	.27g
Saturates	.15g

INGREDIENTS

4 skinless, boneless chicken breasts, about 6 oz/175 g each

salt and pepper

½ cup dry white wine

1–1¼ cups Chicken Stock (see page 13)

1 garlic clove, finely chopped

1 tbsp dried tarragon

¾ cup heavy cream

1 tbsp chopped fresh tarragon

fresh tarragon sprigs, to garnish

cook's tip

Tongs are the easiest way to remove the chicken breasts from the skillet. Make sure that the chicken is completely cooked through before serving.

1 Season the chicken with salt and pepper and place in a single layer in a large, heavy-bottom skillet. Pour in the wine and enough Chicken Stock just to cover and add the garlic and dried tarragon. Bring to a boil, reduce the heat, and poach gently for 10 minutes, or until the chicken is cooked through and tender.

2 Remove the chicken with a slotted spoon or tongs, cover, and keep warm. Strain the poaching liquid into a clean skillet and skim off any fat from the surface. Bring to a boil and cook until reduced by about two-thirds.

3 Stir in the cream, return to a boil, and cook until reduced by about half. Stir in the fresh tarragon. Slice the chicken breasts and arrange on warmed plates. Spoon over the sauce, garnish with tarragon sprigs, and serve immediately.

chicken braised in red wine

⏱ **cook: 27 mins**   ⏲ **prep: 2 mins**   **serves 4**

Rich in color and flavor, this dish needs little in the way of accompaniments except some rustic bread, a little salad, and a glass of the same red wine.

INGREDIENTS

3 tbsp olive oil

4 skinless, boneless chicken breasts, about 5 oz/140 g each

1 red onion, halved and sliced

2 tbsp red pesto

1¼ cups full-bodied red wine

1¼ cups Chicken Stock (see page 13) or water

salt and pepper

⅝ cup seedless red grapes, halved

variation

You can use other cuts of chicken, such as drumsticks and thighs, but meat on the bone may need slightly longer cooking in Step 3.

cook's tip

If time is short, cut the chicken into small strips or cubes, cook over medium heat in Step 1 until cooked through and omit the simmering time in Step 3. Make sure the chicken is piping hot before serving.

1 Heat 2 tablespoons of the olive oil in a large, heavy-bottom skillet or flameproof casserole. Add the chicken and cook over medium heat for 3 minutes on each side, or until golden. Remove from the skillet and set aside until required.

2 Add the remaining olive oil to the skillet. When it is hot, add the onion and pesto and cook over low heat, stirring occasionally, for 5 minutes, or until the onion is softened. Pour in the wine and Chicken Stock and bring to a boil, stirring constantly.

3 Return the chicken to the skillet, season to taste with salt and pepper, cover, and let simmer for 15 minutes, or until the chicken is tender. Add the grapes and heat through for 1 minute. Transfer to warmed dishes and serve immediately.

chicken with green olives

serves 4   **prep: 15 mins** ⏲   **cook: 1 hr 30 mins** ⏲

Olives are a popular flavoring for poultry and game in the Apulia region of Italy, where this traditional recipe originates.

INGREDIENTS

3 tbsp olive oil	6 oz/175 g tomatoes, peeled
2 tbsp butter	and halved
4 chicken breasts, part boned	⅔ cup dry white wine
1 large onion, finely chopped	1 cup pitted green olives
2 garlic cloves, crushed	4–6 tbsp heavy cream
2 red bell peppers, cored, seeded, and	14 oz/400 g dried farfalle
cut into large pieces	salt and pepper
9 oz/250 g white mushrooms,	chopped fresh flatleaf parsley,
sliced or quartered	to garnish

variation

Add a little extra color to this dish by using green and yellow bell peppers instead of the red bell peppers.

cook's tip

Peel the tomatoes by placing them in a bowl and pouring boiling water from the kettle over them. Let stand for 1 minute, then drain and cool under cold running water. The skins should come off easily.

1 Preheat the oven to 350°F/180°C. Place 2 tablespoons of the oil and the butter in a skillet over medium heat. Add the chicken breasts and cook for 3–4 minutes, until golden brown all over. Remove the chicken from the skillet.

2 Add the onion and garlic to the skillet and cook for 1–2 minutes, until starting to soften. Add the bell peppers and mushrooms and cook for 2–3 minutes. Add the tomatoes and season to taste with salt and pepper. Transfer the mixture to a casserole and arrange the chicken on top.

3 Add the wine to the skillet and bring to a boil. Pour the wine over the chicken. Cover and bake in the preheated oven for 50 minutes.

4 Add the olives to the casserole and mix in. Pour in the cream, cover, and return to the oven for 10–20 minutes.

5 Meanwhile, bring a pan of lightly salted water to a boil. Add the pasta and the remaining oil and cook for 8–10 minutes, or until tender but still firm to the bite. Drain and transfer to a serving dish.

6 Serve the chicken and its sauce with the pasta, garnished with parsley.

garlic & herb chicken

serves 4　　　　prep: 20 mins ⏲　　　　cook: 25 mins ⏲

There is a delicious surprise of creamy herb and garlic soft cheese hidden inside these tender chicken packages!

INGREDIENTS

4 chicken breasts, skin removed

generous ⅜ cup whole soft cheese, flavored with herbs and garlic

8 slices prosciutto

⅔ cup red wine

⅔ cup Chicken Stock (see page 13)

1 tbsp brown sugar

NUTRITIONAL INFORMATION

Calories	.272
Protein	.29g
Carbohydrate	.4g
Sugars	.4g
Fat	.13g
Saturates	.6g

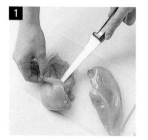

variation

Try adding 2 finely chopped sun-dried tomatoes to the soft cheese in Step 2, if you prefer.

1 Using a sharp knife, make a horizontal slit along the length of each chicken breast to form a wide pocket.

2 Beat the cheese with a wooden spoon to soften it. Spoon the cheese into the pockets of the chicken breasts. Wrap 2 slices of prosciutto round each chicken breast and secure firmly in place with a length of string.

3 Pour the wine and Chicken Stock into a large skillet and bring to a boil. When the mixture is just starting to boil, add the sugar and stir to dissolve.

4 Add the chicken breasts to the mixture in the skillet. Let simmer for 12–15 minutes, or until the chicken is tender and the juices run clear when the tip of a knife is inserted into the thickest part of the meat. Remove the chicken from the skillet with a slotted spoon, set aside, and keep warm.

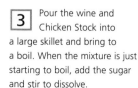

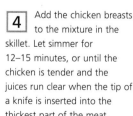

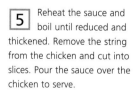

5 Reheat the sauce and boil until reduced and thickened. Remove the string from the chicken and cut into slices. Pour the sauce over the chicken to serve.

chicken cacciatora

⏲ **cook: 1 hr** | 🕐 **prep: 20 mins** | **serves 4**

This is a popular Italian classic in which browned chicken quarters are cooked in a tomato and bell pepper sauce.

NUTRITIONAL INFORMATION

Calories	.397
Protein	.37g
Carbohydrate	.22g
Sugars	.4g
Fat	.17g
Saturates	.4g

INGREDIENTS

1 roasting chicken, about 3 lb 5 oz/
1.5 kg, cut into 6 or 8 serving pieces
generous ¾ cup all-purpose flour
salt and pepper
3 tbsp olive oil
⅔ cup dry white wine
1 green bell pepper, seeded and sliced
1 red bell pepper, seeded and sliced
1 carrot, finely chopped
1 celery stalk, finely chopped
1 garlic clove, crushed
7 oz/200 g canned chopped tomatoes

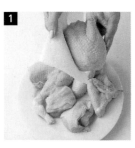

variation

This dish is even more warm and flavorsome if you add an extra clove of crushed garlic.

1 Rinse the chicken pieces and pat dry with paper towels. Place the flour on a plate, season well with salt and pepper, and mix. Lightly dust the chicken pieces with the seasoned flour.

2 Heat the oil in a large skillet. Add the chicken and cook over medium heat for 3–4 minutes, until browned all over. Remove from the skillet with a slotted spoon and set aside.

3 Drain off all but 2 tablespoons of the fat in the skillet. Add the wine and stir for a few minutes, then add the peppers, carrot, celery, and garlic. Season to taste with salt and pepper and let simmer for 15 minutes.

4 Add the chopped tomatoes to the skillet. Cover and let simmer for 30 minutes, stirring frequently, until the chicken is completely cooked through. Check the seasoning before serving piping hot.

This is "OK" but needs pepping up. I added a sprinkling of "Grace" Hot Pepper Sauce. It helped.

Also, I added frozen mushrooms & served over Bistro Fettucine.

butterflied squab chickens

serves 4   **prep: 15 mins** (╵   **cook: 12 mins**

The perfect alternative to roast chicken when you find yourself short of time or fancy a change, these little birds are simply split open and broiled.

INGREDIENTS

4 squab chickens

2 oz/55 g butter

1 tbsp lemon juice

1 tbsp chopped fresh parsley, plus extra to garnish

1 tsp chopped fresh tarragon

salt and pepper

mixed salad greens, to serve

NUTRITIONAL INFORMATION	
Calories	.470
Protein	.39g
Carbohydrate	.0g
Sugars	.0g
Fat	.35g
Saturates	.15g

variation

Omit the herbs and stir 1 tablespoon mustard powder, 1 tablespoon paprika, and 1 tablespoon Worcestershire sauce into the melted butter for a spicy dish.

cook's tip

You can thread the skewers crosswise through the squab chickens, if you like. Push a skewer through a wing and out through the thigh on the opposite side. Repeat with the other skewer on the other side.

1 Preheat the broiler to high. If the squab chickens are trussed, remove and discard the string. Using kitchen scissors, cut along either side of the backbone of each bird and remove. Lay the squab chickens down and flatten with a rolling pin or the heel of your hand. Thread a

long skewer from wing to wing and from leg to leg through each bird to keep them flat.

2 Melt the butter, brush it over the squab chickens and set aside the remainder. Sprinkle with lemon juice, parsley, and tarragon and season with salt and pepper.

3 Place the squab chickens on a broiler rack, skin-side uppermost, and cook under the preheated broiler for 6 minutes, or until golden. Turn them over, brush with the remaining melted butter and broil for an additional 6 minutes, or until cooked through. Remove the

skewers and transfer to warmed serving plates. Garnish with extra parsley and serve immediately with mixed salad greens.

fish & shellfish

Fish is the busy cook's best friend—versatile, tasty, healthy, and quick to cook. Nutritionists recommend that we should eat fish at least twice a week and this superb collection of delicious and speedy recipes is just what the doctor ordered. Dishes range from familiar favorites and classic dishes, such as Trout with Almonds (see page 176), Sole Meunière (see page 183), and Thai Shrimp Curry (see page 202), to more unusual and contemporary recipes, such as Blackened Fish (see page 174), Angler Fish in a Ruby Grapefruit Sauce (see page 179), and Catalan Mussels (see page 208). There are tasty midweek suppers, such as Finnan Haddie (see page 177) and Mediterranean Cod (see page 184), and sophisticated dinner-party dishes, such as Lobster Thermidor (see page 193) and Thai Fragrant Mussels (see page 209). Your guests will never believe that you "just threw it together in a few minutes after work."

Inspiration comes from across the world, with recipes from places as far apart as France, Pakistan, Italy, Scotland, Thailand, and Mexico, and all kinds of fish and shellfish are featured, from cod to red snapper and from scallops to salmon. Whatever your tastes, from fiery hot Balti Shrimp (see page 203) to satisfying Haddock in a Cheese Jacket (see page 173) and from the elegant simplicity of Salmon with Watercress Cream (see page 180) to tasty baked Crab Creole (see page 197), you can be sure that the world is your oyster.

haddock in a cheese jacket

cook: 12–15 mins   **prep: 15 mins**   **serves 4**

Rather than a cheese sauce, these fish fillets are smothered in a more unusual cheese-flavored paste that gives them a lovely golden jacket, making them especially popular with children.

INGREDIENTS

2 tbsp olive oil, plus extra for brushing

4 haddock fillets, about

6 oz/175 g each

grated rind and juice of 2 lemons

salt and pepper

4 oz/115 g Swiss cheese, grated

4 tbsp fresh white bread crumbs

4 tbsp sour cream

4 garlic cloves, finely chopped

TO GARNISH

lemon wedges

fresh parsley sprigs

variation

You could use any white fish fillets, such as cod, coley, whiting, or hake, if you prefer.

cook's tip

It is quite easy to overcook fish. When the fish is done, the flesh should be opaque nearly all the way through and it should flake easily when tested with a fork.

1 Preheat the oven to 400°F/200°C. Brush a roasting pan or large ovenproof dish with olive oil and arrange the fish in it in a single layer. Sprinkle with a little lemon juice and season to taste with salt and pepper.

2 Mix the olive oil, cheese, bread crumbs, sour cream, garlic, lemon rind, and 6 tablespoons of the remaining lemon juice together in a large bowl and season to taste with salt and pepper. Spread the cheese paste evenly over the fish fillets.

3 Bake in the preheated oven for 12–15 minutes, or until the fish is cooked through. Transfer to warmed serving plates, garnish with lemon wedges, and parsley sprigs, and serve immediately.

blackened fish

serves 4   **prep: 10 mins** ◔   **cook: 6–8 mins** ◔

Contrary to popular opinion, this fashionable Cajun dish is not the least bit traditional and was first created at the end of the twentieth century.

INGREDIENTS

1 tsp black peppercorns	2 tbsp cornmeal
1 tsp fennel seeds	4 angler fish fillets, about
1 tsp cayenne pepper	6 oz/175 g each, skinned
1 tsp dried oregano	3 tbsp corn oil
1 tsp dried thyme	
3 garlic cloves, finely chopped	TO GARNISH
	thinly pared strips of lime rind
	lime halves

NUTRITIONAL INFORMATION

Calories 225

Protein 29g

Carbohydrate 7g

Sugars 0g

Fat 10g

Saturates 1g

variation

Use this spice mixture for blackened chicken. Coat 4 skinless, boneless chicken breasts, about 6 oz/175 g each. Cook for 3 minutes each side.

cook's tip

If you would like a spicier flavor, then rub the Cajun spice mix into the flesh of the fish and let stand for 10–15 minutes. Proceed from Step 3 in main recipe.

1 Crush the peppercorns lightly in a mortar with a pestle. Mix the peppercorns, fennel seeds, cayenne, oregano, thyme, garlic, and cornmeal in a shallow dish.

2 Place the angler fish, 1 fillet at a time, in the spice mixture and press gently to coat all over. Shake off any excess.

3 Heat the corn oil in a large, heavy-bottom skillet. Add the angler fish and cook for 3–4 minutes on each side, or until tender and cooked through. Serve garnished with the lime rind and lime halves.

trout with almonds

serves 2   **prep: 5 mins**   **cook: 15–20 mins**

The simple elegance and delicate flavor of this classic combination ensures its continuing popularity. Serve with new potatoes and freshly cooked broccoli for a delicious meal at any time.

INGREDIENTS

generous ¼ cup all-purpose flour

salt and pepper

2 trout, about 12 oz/350 g

each, cleaned

2 oz/55 g butter

¼ cup slivered almonds

2 tbsp dry white wine

NUTRITIONAL INFORMATION

Calories	700
Protein	. . . . .59g
Carbohydrate	. . . . .17g
Sugars	. . . . .1g
Fat	. . . . .44g
Saturates	. . . . .19g

variation

Substitute either rainbow trout or salmon for the trout, if you prefer.

1 Spread the flour out on a large, flat plate and season to taste with salt and pepper. Coat the trout in the seasoned flour, shaking off any excess.

2 Melt half the butter in a large, heavy-bottom skillet. Add the fish and cook over medium heat for 6–7 minutes on each side, or until tender and cooked through. Transfer the trout to warmed plates with a spatula, cover, and keep warm.

3 Melt the remaining butter in the skillet. Add the almonds and cook, stirring frequently, for 2 minutes, or until golden brown. Add the wine, bring to a boil and boil for 1 minute. Spoon the almonds and sauce over the trout and serve immediately.

finnan haddie

cook: 20 mins   **prep: 5 mins**   **serves 4**

Finnan haddock is, in fact, a small whole haddock that has been soaked in brine before cold smoking. However, you can use undyed smoked haddock fillet for this traditional Scottish dish.

NUTRITIONAL INFORMATION

Calories	.320
Protein	.33g
Carbohydrate	.4g
Sugars	.4g
Fat	.19g
Saturates	.10g

INGREDIENTS

1 lb 2 oz/500 g smoked haddock,
skinned and cut into chunks

1 cup milk

½ cup light cream

2 tbsp unsalted butter

pepper

4 eggs

cook's tip

Look for undyed, smoked haddock, which is a more attractive color, has a better flavor, and is healthier. It is usually available from most supermarkets.

1 Preheat the oven to 350°F/180°C. Place the chunks of fish in a large ovenproof dish. Pour the milk and cream into a small pan, add the butter, season to taste with pepper and heat gently until the butter has melted. Pour the mixture over the fish.

2 Bake in the preheated oven for 20 minutes, or until the fish is tender.

3 Meanwhile, bring a small pan of water to a boil. Break an egg into a cup, stir the water to create a small "whirlpool," and slide in the egg. Poach for

3–4 minutes, or until the white is set, but the yolk is still soft. Remove and drain, trimming any stray strings of white, if necessary. Poach the remaining eggs in the same way. Top the dish of fish with the eggs and serve immediately.

angler fish in a ruby grapefruit sauce

cook: 15 mins   **prep: 10 mins**   **serves 4**

Angler fish fillets are always a good choice for a fish dish because there are no irritating little pin bones and the delicious flesh has a meaty texture.

INGREDIENTS

2 tbsp butter

1 lb 12 oz/800 g angler fish fillets, cut into chunks

2 tbsp lemon juice

salt and pepper

3 carrots, thinly sliced

juice of 2 ruby grapefruit

4 tbsp heavy cream

generous ⅓ cup fish stock

1 tbsp corn oil

1 ruby grapefruit, cut into segments, to garnish

variation

Substitute the fish stock with Chicken Stock (see page 13), if you prefer, and replace the ruby grapefruit with 1 large orange.

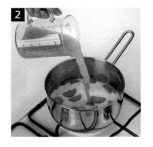

cook's tip

Angler fish is usually sold skinned, but sometimes the transparent gray membrane that surrounds the flesh is still in place. Peel this off before cutting and cooking the fish.

1 Melt half the butter in a large, heavy-bottom skillet. Sprinkle the fish with the lemon juice, season to taste with salt and pepper, then add to the skillet and cook over medium heat for 2½–3 minutes on each side.

2 Meanwhile, melt the remaining butter in a heavy-bottom pan. Add the carrots and cook over low heat, stirring frequently, for 10 minutes, or until tender. Stir in the grapefruit juice, cream, fish stock, and oil, and let simmer for 5 minutes. Remove the pan from the heat and let cool slightly.

3 Transfer the carrot and grapefruit mixture to a blender or food processor and process until a smooth purée forms. Season to taste with salt and pepper. Spoon the sauce onto 4 warmed plates, top with the angler fish chunks, garnish with the grapefruit segments, and serve.

salmon with watercress cream

serves 4   **prep: 5 mins**   **cook: 20 mins**

*Once a luxurious and expensive treat, salmon is now widely
available at an affordable price as a result of fish farming.
However, if you have the chance to buy wild salmon, do so,
as it has an incomparable flavor and a finer texture.*

INGREDIENTS

1¼ cups sour cream

2 tbsp chopped fresh dill

2 tbsp unsalted butter

1 tbsp corn oil

4 salmon fillets, about 6 oz/175 g
each, skinned

1 garlic clove, finely chopped

generous ⅓ cup dry white wine

1 bunch of watercress, finely chopped

salt and pepper

variation

If watercress is unavailable, then
replace with the same amount of
arugula or baby spinach leaves.

cook's tip

Fresh dill goes particularly well
with fish, especially salmon,
as it has a delicate aniseed
flavor. It cannot withstand
high temperatures, so is best
used at the end of cooking or
as a garnish.

1 Pour the sour cream into a large, heavy-bottom pan and heat gently to simmering point. Remove the pan from the heat, stir in the dill, and set aside.

2 Melt the butter with the corn oil in a heavy-bottom skillet. Add the salmon fillets and cook over medium heat for 4–5 minutes on each side, or until cooked through. Remove the fish from the skillet, cover, and keep warm.

3 Add the garlic to the skillet and cook, stirring, for 1 minute. Pour in the white wine, bring to a boil and cook until reduced. Stir the sour cream mixture into the skillet and cook for 2–3 minutes, or until thickened.

4 Stir in the watercress and cook until just wilted. Season to taste with salt and pepper. Place the salmon fillets on warmed serving plates, spoon the watercress sauce over them, and serve immediately.

sole meunière

⏲ **cook: 12 mins**   ⏱ **prep: 5 mins**   **serves 4**

variation

A classic variation is Sole aux Légumes Poêles, in which the fish is served with pan fried vegetables, such as red bell pepper, cucumber, and eggplant.

Sole has a delicate and subtle flavor, so it is best cooked very simply, rather than being smothered in a rich sauce. This classic French recipe is the best way to do it.

INGREDIENTS

1 cup milk

¾ cup all-purpose flour

salt and pepper

1 lb 9 oz/700 g sole fillets

2 tbsp butter

1–2 tbsp corn oil

2 tbsp chopped fresh parsley

lemon wedges, to garnish

cook's tip

In spite of their shared name, lemon sole is unrelated to the Dover sole, which is only found in European waters. It is rather a shame because it suffers by comparison, yet is a tasty fish in its own right.

1 Pour the milk into a large, shallow dish. Place the flour on a large, flat plate and season to taste with salt and pepper.

2 Dip the sole in the milk and then in the flour, turning to coat. Shake off any excess.

3 Melt the butter with the corn oil in a large, heavy-bottom skillet. Add the fish fillets, in batches, and cook over low heat for 2–3 minutes on each side, or until lightly browned. Keep each batch warm in a low oven while you cook the remaining fish, then sprinkle with the chopped parsley and serve immediately, garnished with the lemon wedges.

mediterranean cod

serves 4   **prep: 10 mins** ⟳   **cook: 15 mins** ⟳

This is a perfect example of the healthy Mediterranean diet that nutritionists recommend—and what is more, it tastes fabulous. Serve with a fresh, crisp salad for a delicious lunch.

INGREDIENTS

14 oz/400 g canned chopped tomatoes

1 garlic clove, finely chopped

1 tbsp sun-dried tomato paste

1 tbsp Pernod

1 tbsp capers, drained and rinsed

⅓ cup black olives, pitted

salt and pepper

4 cod steaks, about 6 oz/175 g each

⅔ cup dry white wine

1 bay leaf

¼ tsp black peppercorns

thinly pared strip of lemon rind

fresh flatleaf parsley sprigs,
to garnish

NUTRITIONAL INFORMATION

Calories 219

Protein 33g

Carbohydrate 4g

Sugars 3g

Fat 4g

Saturates 1g

1 Place the chopped tomatoes, garlic, tomato paste, Pernod, capers, and olives in a large, heavy-bottom pan and season to taste with salt and pepper. Heat gently, stirring occasionally.

2 Meanwhile, place the cod steaks in a single layer in a large, heavy-bottom skillet and pour the wine over them. Add the bay leaf, peppercorns, and lemon rind, and bring to a boil. Reduce the heat, cover. and let simmer for 10 minutes, or until the fish is tender.

3 Transfer the cod to a warmed serving dish with a spatula. Strain the cooking liquid into the tomato mixture and bring to a boil. Boil for 1–2 minutes, or until slightly reduced and thickened, then spoon the sauce over the fish. Garnish with parsley sprigs and serve immediately.

cook's tip

Use a vegetable peeler to pare a thin strip of lemon rind from a lemon. The recipe uses fresh flatleaf parsley rather than curly for the garnish, as it has a more pronounced flavor.

skate in black butter sauce

 cook: 10–15 mins   prep: 5 mins   serves 4

The title of this classic recipe is misleading, as butter that has turned black is burnt and quite disgusting. In fact, it should be a delicious brown color that complements the sweet flesh of the skate.

NUTRITIONAL INFORMATION	
Calories	.229
Protein	.21g
Carbohydrate	.1g
Sugars	.1g
Fat	.12g
Saturates	.7g

INGREDIENTS

1 lb 8 oz/675 g skate wings

2½ cups fish stock

1 cup dry white wine

salt and pepper

2 oz/55 g butter

2 tbsp lemon juice

2 tsp capers, drained and rinsed

2 tbsp chopped fresh parsley

cook's tip

Skate is not at its best when freshly caught, but its flavor improves with keeping for 2–3 days. It may have a smell of ammonia—removed by rinsing and patting dry. If the smell is strong, don't buy it.

1 Place the fish in a large, heavy-bottom skillet or flameproof casserole, pour in the fish stock and wine, and season to taste with salt and pepper. Bring to a boil, reduce the heat, and let simmer for 10–15 minutes, or until the fish is tender.

2 Meanwhile, melt the butter in a separate large, heavy-based skillet and cook over very low heat until it turns brown, but not black. Stir in the lemon juice, capers, and parsley and heat for an additional 1–2 minutes.

3 Transfer the skate wings to warmed serving plates with a spatula, pour the black butter sauce over them, and serve.

veracruz red snapper

serves 4   **prep: 5 mins, plus** ⟳
30 mins marinating   **cook: 25 mins** ⟳

One of Mexico's most popular dishes, this looks, smells and tastes out of this world and would be a perfect choice as a main course for a dinner party.

INGREDIENTS

4 red snapper fillets	pinch of dried marjoram
salt and pepper	⅓ cup green olives, pitted
2 tbsp lime juice	and halved
½ cup corn oil	2 tbsp capers, drained and rinsed
1 onion, chopped	2 pickled green chiles, drained, seeded,
2 garlic cloves, finely chopped	and sliced
1 lb 8 oz/675 g tomatoes, peeled	2 oz/55 g butter
and chopped	3 slices white bread, crusts removed
1 bay leaf	

NUTRITIONAL INFORMATION

Calories	.557
Protein	.37g
Carbohydrate	.15g
Sugars	.7g
Fat	.39g
Saturates	.11g

variation

Replace the red snapper with pompano and if you prefer, use vegetable oil instead of the corn oil.

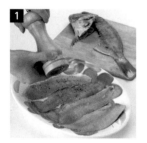

cook's tip

Adding lime or lemon juice to fish helps to make the flesh tender, but don't leave the fish too long in the lime juice, otherwise the juice will start to cook the fish.

1 Place the red snapper fillets in a large, shallow, nonmetallic dish in a single layer and season to taste with salt and pepper. Pour the lime juice over them and let marinate until required.

2 Heat the corn oil in a large, heavy-bottom skillet. Add the onion and garlic and cook over low heat, stirring occasionally, for 5 minutes, or until the onion has softened. Add the chopped tomatoes and cook, stirring occasionally, for an additional 10 minutes, or until thickened and pulpy. Stir in the bay leaf, dried marjoram, green olives, capers, and chiles, and add the fish fillets. Cook for 10 minutes, or until the fish is tender.

3 Meanwhile, melt the butter in a separate skillet. Cut the bread into triangles and cook for 2–3 minutes on each side, or until golden brown. Drain on paper towels. Remove and discard the bay leaf from the fish and vegetables. Transfer to a warmed serving dish, garnish with the cooked bread, and serve immediately.

noodles with chile & shrimp

serves 4　　　　**prep: 10 mins** ⏱　　　　**cook: 5 mins** ⏱

This is a simple dish to prepare and is packed with flavor, making it an ideal, easy-to-make dish for special occasions.

INGREDIENTS

9 oz/250 g thin glass noodles

2 tbsp corn oil

1 onion, sliced

2 red chiles, seeded and very finely chopped

4 lime leaves, thinly shredded

1 tbsp fresh cilantro

2 tbsp jaggery or superfine sugar

2 tbsp nam pla (Thai fish sauce)

1 lb/450 g raw jumbo shrimp, shelled and deveined

variation

You can use ordinary cooked prawns instead of the jumbo shrimp, if you like. Cook them with the noodles for 1 minute only, to heat through.

cook's tip

Glass noodles, also known as bean thread noodles or cellophane noodles, are made from mung bean starch. They are available from Asian food stores and large supermarkets.

 1 Place the noodles in a large bowl. Pour over enough boiling water to cover and let stand for 5 minutes. Drain thoroughly and set aside until required.

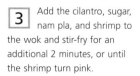 **2** Place a wok or skillet over high heat until warm, then add the corn oil and heat until really hot. Add the onion, red chiles, and lime leaves to the wok and stir-fry for 1 minute.

3 Add the cilantro, sugar, nam pla, and shrimp to the wok and stir-fry for an additional 2 minutes, or until the shrimp turn pink.

4 Add the drained noodles to the wok, toss to mix well, and stir-fry for 1–2 minutes, or until heated through. Transfer the noodles and shrimp to warmed serving bowls and serve immediately.

scallops on skewers

serves 4   **prep: 10 mins** ⏲   **cook: 8 mins** ⏲

Scallops can easily be overcooked, when they become unpleasantly tough. However, they are an ideal choice for the busy cook. This simple dish, which can be cooked under the broiler or on a barbecue, will serve four people as a main course or eight as an appetizer.

INGREDIENTS

48 prepared scallops,
thawed if frozen
juice of 1 lemon
24 slices of prosciutto
olive oil, for brushing
mixed salad greens
pepper
lemon wedges, to garnish

NUTRITIONAL INFORMATION

Calories	.498
Protein	.80g
Carbohydrate	.8g
Sugars	.0g
Fat	.16g
Saturates	.5g

cook's tip

The corals, or roe, are not used in this dish. It is an interesting cultural difference that the corals are prized in Europe but not eaten in the United States.

1 Preheat the broiler to medium. Sprinkle the scallops with the lemon juice. Cut the prosciutto into strips, then wrap a strip round each scallop and thread them onto presoaked wooden skewers, 3–4 at a time.

2 Brush the scallops with olive oil and place them on a large baking sheet. Cook under the preheated broiler for 4 minutes on each side, or until the scallops are opaque and tender.

3 Make a bed of mixed salad greens on individual serving plates and divide the skewers between them. Season to taste with pepper, garnish with lemon wedges, and serve.

broiled scallops & shrimp with citrus butter

⏲ cook: 8–9 mins   ⏱ prep: 10 mins   serves 4

Seafood and citrus fruit have a natural affinity with each other and this dish will taste equally delicious whether you use limes or lemons to flavor the butter. Unshelled shrimp look attractive, but you can shell them, if you like.

NUTRITIONAL INFORMATION

Calories	.337
Protein	.25g
Carbohydrate	.9g
Sugars	.4g
Fat	.23g
Saturates	.13g

INGREDIENTS

12 prepared scallops, thawed if frozen

12 raw jumbo shrimp

finely grated rind and juice of 1 lime
or lemon

1 egg yolk

6 tbsp melted butter

1 tbsp chopped fresh dill or chopped
fresh chervil

salt and pepper

2 red onions, cut into wedges

olive oil, for brushing

cook's tip

If using wooden skewers, soak them in warm water for 30 minutes, drain, pat dry, then thread the food onto them. Soaking prevents the skewers burning under the broiler or on the barbecue.

1 Preheat the broiler to medium. Place the scallops and shrimp in a large, shallow, nonmetallic dish, add half the citrus rind and half the juice and toss well.

2 Beat the egg yolk with the remaining citrus rind and juice in a small bowl. Gradually whisk in the melted butter, 1 tablespoon at a time.

Continue to whisk until the mixture is thick and smooth. Stir in the dill and season to taste with salt and pepper.

3 Brush the onion wedges with olive oil and cook under the preheated broiler for 5 minutes, turning them once. Meanwhile, thread the scallops and shrimp onto presoaked wooden skewers, add them

to the broiler and cook for 1½–2 minutes on each side, or until the scallops are opaque and the shrimp have changed color.

4 Remove the seafood from the skewers and place on a warmed serving plate. Surround them with the onion wedges, pour the citrus butter over them, and serve.

lobster thermidor

cook: 15 mins   **prep: 15 mins**   **serves 4**

A little extravagant, but this is the perfect dish for an extra special occasion and is guaranteed to impress.

INGREDIENTS

2 cooked lobsters, about 1 lb 10 oz/750 g each

2 oz/55 g butter

1 shallot, chopped

scant ¼ cup all-purpose flour

1¼ cups milk

1½ tsp chopped fresh chervil

1 tsp chopped fresh tarragon

1½ tsp chopped fresh parsley

2 tsp Dijon mustard

salt and pepper

6 tbsp dry white wine

3 tbsp heavy cream

4 tbsp freshly grated Parmesan cheese

TO GARNISH

lemon slices

fresh parsley sprigs

variation

Lobster Newburg has a richer sauce, as it is made with heavy cream and egg yolk. Use Madeira instead of wine and ¼ teaspoon cayenne instead of herbs.

cook's tip

You can polish the half-shells of the lobster with a few drops of olive oil to make the dish look even more attractive, if you like.

1 Preheat the broiler to medium. Twist off and discard the lobster heads and pull off the claws. Crack the claws with a small hammer and remove the flesh. Using a sharp knife, split the lobsters in half lengthwise and remove and discard the intestinal vein. Remove the flesh and set aside. Scrub the half-shells under cold running water and drain upside down on paper towels. Cut the lobster flesh into ¾-inch/2-cm thick slices.

2 Melt the butter in a heavy-bottom pan. Add the shallot and cook over low heat for 4–5 minutes, or until softened. Sprinkle in the flour and cook, stirring constantly, for 2 minutes. Remove the pan from the heat and gradually stir in the milk. Return the pan to the heat and bring to a boil, stirring. Cook, stirring, until thickened and smooth.

3 Reduce the heat, stir in the herbs, and mustard, and season to taste with salt and pepper. Remove the pan from the heat and whisk in the wine and cream. Return to low heat and let simmer until thickened. Add the lobster flesh and heat through for 2–3 minutes.

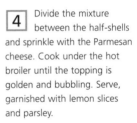

4 Divide the mixture between the half-shells and sprinkle with the Parmesan cheese. Cook under the hot broiler until the topping is golden and bubbling. Serve, garnished with lemon slices and parsley.

shrimp in anchovy sauce

serves 4   **prep: 10 mins** ⟲   **cook: 15 mins** ⏲

Finger bowls and napkins are essential accessories for eating these tasty but rather messy shrimp. Crusty bread will help mop up all the delicious juices.

INGREDIENTS

6 tbsp olive oil

4 garlic cloves, finely chopped

5 canned anchovy fillets, drained and chopped

3 tbsp finely chopped fresh flatleaf parsley

6 tbsp dry white wine

14 oz/400 g canned chopped tomatoes

pinch of chili powder

salt and pepper

3 lb 5 oz/1.5 kg large raw shrimp, unshelled

TO GARNISH

lemon wedges

fresh flatleaf parsley sprigs

NUTRITIONAL INFORMATION

Calories 347

Protein 35g

Carbohydrate 4g

Sugars 3g

Fat 20g

Saturates 3g

---

variation

Replace the lemon wedges with lime wedges and use chopped, peeled, and seeded fresh tomatoes instead of canned, if you prefer.

cook's tip

When buying shrimp, always choose ones that look and smell fresh, and that have shiny shells. Jumbo shrimp are the best choice for this dish.

1 Heat the olive oil in a large, heavy-bottom pan. Add the garlic, anchovies, and parsley and cook, stirring frequently, for 5 minutes. Add the wine and cook, stirring constantly, until reduced.

2 Add the tomatoes with their can juices and the chili powder and season to taste with salt and pepper. Add the shrimp, reduce the heat, and let simmer gently for 10 minutes, or until the shrimp have changed color.

3 Divide the shrimp and sauce between warmed serving dishes, garnish with lemon wedges and parsley sprigs, and serve immediately.

gamberi fritti

serves 4   **prep: 5 mins** ⏲   **cook: 10 mins** ⏲

Like most Italian dishes, the keynotes of these shrimp are simplicity and the best-quality ingredients. Gamberi are large, Mediterranean shrimp with a fine flavor, but any fresh shrimp may be used.

INGREDIENTS

4 tbsp olive oil

32 large raw shrimp, unshelled

3 garlic cloves, finely chopped

½ cup dry white vermouth

3 tbsp strained tomatoes

salt and pepper

3 tbsp chopped fresh

flatleaf parsley

NUTRITIONAL INFORMATION

Calories	209
Protein	. . . . .15g
Carbohydrate	. . . . .3g
Sugars	. . . . .2g
Fat	. . . . .12g
Saturates	. . . . .2g

cook's tip

Shrimp are cooked as soon as they turn pink. Large, unshelled shrimp may take slightly longer to cook. To test if they are done, cut a shrimp in half and if the flesh is opaque, then they are cooked.

1 Heat the olive oil in a large, heavy-bottom pan. Add the shrimp and cook over high heat, stirring and tossing constantly, until they change color.

2 Add the garlic and vermouth and cook, stirring and tossing the shrimp constantly, until the liquid comes to a boil.

3 Add the strained tomatoes and season to taste with salt and pepper. Stir the shrimp until they are thoroughly coated. Transfer to warmed serving plates, sprinkle with the chopped parsley, and serve immediately.

crab creole

cook: 20 mins   **prep: 10 mins**   **serves 6**

You can use fresh, frozen and thawed, or canned crabmeat for this recipe. You could also substitute the sherry with dry white wine, if you prefer.

NUTRITIONAL INFORMATION

Calories	349
Protein	. . . . .18g
Carbohydrate	. . . . .5g
Sugars	. . . . .1g
Fat	. . . . .28g
Saturates	. . . . .15g

INGREDIENTS

3 hard-cooked eggs, shelled

1 tsp Dijon mustard

3 tbsp butter

¼ tsp cayenne pepper

3 tbsp dry sherry

1 tbsp chopped fresh dill

14 oz/400 g crabmeat

⅓ cup heavy cream

3 scallions, thinly sliced

salt and pepper

½ cup dried white bread crumbs

cook's tip

For perfect cooked eggs, bring the eggs to room temperature, then bring a pan of water to a boil. Reduce the heat and cook the eggs for 12 minutes. Plunge in cold water and leave for 8 minutes before shelling.

1 Preheat the oven to 350°F/180°C. Separate the hard-cooked egg whites and yolks. Place the yolks in a small bowl and mash lightly with a fork. Add the mustard, 2 oz/55 g of the butter and the cayenne pepper, and mash to a paste. Stir in the sherry and dill.

2 Flake the crabmeat into a separate small bowl, removing any pieces of shell or cartilage. Chop the egg whites and stir them into the crabmeat with the cream and scallions. Season to taste with salt and pepper.

3 Divide the mixture between 6 individual ovenproof dishes. Sprinkle with the bread crumbs and dot with the remaining butter. Bake in the preheated oven for 20 minutes, or until the topping is golden brown. Serve immediately.

fillets of red snapper & pasta

serves 4   prep: 15 mins ⟳   cook: 1 hour ⟳

A simple mixture of garlic, herbs, lemon, nutmeg, and anchovies perfectly complements the sweet, delicate flesh of red snapper.

INGREDIENTS

2 lb 4 oz/1 kg red snapper fillets
1¼ cups dry white wine
4 shallots, finely chopped
1 garlic clove, crushed
3 tbsp finely chopped mixed
fresh herbs
finely grated rind and juice of 1 lemon
pinch of freshly grated nutmeg
3 anchovy fillets, coarsely chopped
salt and pepper

2 tbsp heavy cream
1 tsp cornstarch
1 lb/450 g dried vermicelli
1 tbsp olive oil

TO GARNISH
1 fresh mint sprig
lemon slices
lemon rind

variation

You can substitute red snapper for pompano, and if you like garlic, add a small extra clove, crushed.

cook's tip

Remember to protect your hands when you transfer the casserole from the oven to the stove—the handles will be hot—and be careful not to burn your kitchen counter by resting the hot dish on it.

1 Preheat the oven to 350°F/180°C. Place the red snapper fillets in a large casserole. Pour over the wine and add the shallots, garlic, herbs, lemon rind and juice, nutmeg, and anchovies. Season to taste with salt and pepper, then cover and bake in the preheated oven for 35 minutes.

2 Transfer the snapper to a warmed dish with a wooden spoon. Set aside and keep warm.

3 Place the casserole on the stove over high heat and bring the cooking liquid to a boil. Reduce the heat and let simmer for

25 minutes, until reduced by half. Mix the cream and cornstarch and stir into the sauce to thicken.

4 Meanwhile, bring a large pan of lightly salted water to a boil. Add the vermicelli and oil and cook for 8–10 minutes, until tender but

still firm to the bite. Drain the pasta and transfer to a warmed serving dish.

5 Arrange the red snapper fillets on top of the vermicelli and pour over the sauce. Garnish with a fresh mint sprig, slices of lemon, and strips of lemon rind and serve.

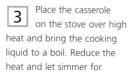

trout with smoked bacon

serves 4   **prep: 35 mins** ⟲   **cook: 25 mins** ⟳

Most trout available nowadays is farmed rainbow trout, however,
if you can, buy wild brown trout for this recipe.

INGREDIENTS

1 tbsp butter, for greasing

4 trout, about 9½ oz/275 g
each, cleaned

salt and pepper

12 anchovies in oil, drained
and chopped

2 apples, peeled, cored, and sliced

4 fresh mint sprigs

juice of 1 lemon

12 slices rindless smoked fatty bacon

1 lb/450 g dried tagliatelle

1 tbsp olive oil

TO GARNISH

2 apples, cored and sliced

4 fresh mint sprigs

NUTRITIONAL INFORMATION	
Calories	.802
Protein	.68g
Carbohydrate	.54g
Sugars	.8g
Fat	.36g
Saturates	.10g

variation

Replace the mint sprigs with another fresh herb of your choice, if you like. Parsley also works well in this recipe.

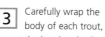

cook's tip

Use eating apples such as Baldwins or Braeburn apples for this dish. Place the apple slices in cold water mixed with a little lemon juice to prevent them browning while you prepare the rest of the recipe.

1 Preheat the oven to 400°F/200°C. Grease a deep baking sheet with the butter.

2 Open up the cavities of each trout and rinse with warm salt water. Season each cavity with salt and pepper. Divide the anchovies, sliced apples, and mint sprigs between each of the cavities. Sprinkle the lemon juice into each cavity.

3 Carefully wrap the body of each trout, except the head and tail, with 3 slices of smoked bacon wound in a spiral. Arrange the trout on the prepared baking sheet with the loose ends of bacon tucked underneath. Season with pepper and bake in the preheated oven for 20 minutes, turning the trout over after 10 minutes.

4 Meanwhile, bring a large pan of lightly salted water to a boil. Add the tagliatelle and olive oil and cook for 12 minutes, or until tender but still firm to the bite. Drain the pasta and transfer to a large, warmed serving dish.

5 Remove the trout from the oven and arrange on the tagliatelle. Garnish with sliced apples and fresh mint sprigs, and serve immediately.

thai shrimp curry

serves 4   **prep: 10 mins** ⟲   **cook: 10 mins** ⏱

Jumbo shrimp are cooked in a fragrant mixture of green curry paste, herbs, and coconut milk to produce a tasty meal in minutes.

INGREDIENTS

2 tbsp peanut oil

2 tbsp Thai green curry paste

4 kaffir lime leaves, shredded

1 lemon grass stalk, crushed and finely chopped

1 lb/450 g raw jumbo shrimp, shelled and deveined

1 cup coconut milk

2 tbsp Thai fish sauce

½ cucumber, seeded and cut into thin sticks

12 fresh basil leaves

4 fresh green chiles, seeded and sliced

NUTRITIONAL INFORMATION

Calories	.216
Protein	.27g
Carbohydrate	.5g
Sugars	.3g
Fat	.10g
Saturates	.2g

cook's tip

Lemon grass stalks, available in Asian food stores and some supermarkets, are used widely in Southeast Asia. To prepare a stalk, remove and discard the outer layer, crush with a rolling pin, and chop or slice.

1 Heat the peanut oil in a preheated wok or large, heavy-bottom skillet. Add the curry paste and cook, stirring frequently, until it gives off its aroma and is starting to bubble. Add the lime leaves, lemon grass, and shrimp, and stir-fry for 2 minutes, or until the shrimp are starting to change color.

2 Pour in the coconut milk, stir gently, then bring the mixture to a boil. Reduce the heat and let simmer, stirring occasionally, for 5 minutes, or until the shrimp are tender.

3 Stir in the Thai fish sauce, cucumber sticks, basil leaves, and sliced chiles. Transfer to warmed serving dishes and serve immediately.

balti shrimp

cook: 10 mins　　　**prep: 10 mins**　　　**serves 4**

*This curry is not for the faint-hearted, as it is fiery hot. Serve with
naan bread and a cooling cucumber raita to soothe the taste buds.*

NUTRITIONAL INFORMATION

Calories 180

Protein 16g

Carbohydrate 8g

Sugars 6g

Fat 10g

Saturates 1g

INGREDIENTS

4 fresh green chiles

2 onions, coarsely chopped

2 tbsp lemon juice

2 tbsp tomato paste

3 tbsp chopped fresh cilantro

1 tsp ground coriander

1 tsp chili powder

½ tsp ground turmeric

pinch of salt

1 tbsp water (optional)

3 tbsp corn oil

**32 large raw shrimp, shelled
and deveined**

cook's tip

For a cucumber raita, beat
1¼ cups plain yogurt, then
stir in ¼ diced cucumber,
1 chopped fresh chile,
¼ teaspoon ground cumin and
salt to taste. Let chill in the
refrigerator before serving.

1 Seed and thinly slice
2 of the chiles and set
aside for the garnish. Place
the whole chiles, onions,
lemon juice, tomato paste,
2 tablespoons of the fresh
cilantro, the ground coriander,
chili powder, turmeric, and salt
in a food processor and
process until a smooth paste
forms. If necessary, thin with
the water.

2 Heat the corn oil in a
preheated wok or large,
heavy-bottom skillet. Add the
spice paste and cook, stirring
constantly, for 4 minutes, or
until thickened.

3 Add the shrimp and
cook, stirring constantly,
for 4–5 minutes, or until they
have changed color. Transfer
to a warmed serving plate,
garnish with the sliced chiles
and remaining fresh cilantro,
and serve immediately.

shrimp pasta bake

serves 4　　　　**prep: 10 mins** ⏲　　　　**cook: 50 mins** ⏲

This recipe is ideal for a substantial supper. You can use whatever pasta you like, but the tricolor varieties will give colorful results, and make the dish look especially tempting.

INGREDIENTS

8 oz/225 g dried tricolor pasta shapes

1 tbsp vegetable oil

6 oz/175 g white mushrooms, sliced

1 bunch scallions, trimmed and chopped

salmon (pink)

14 oz/400 g canned tuna in brine, drained and flaked

6 oz/175 g cooked shelled shrimp, thawed if frozen

2 tbsp cornstarch

generous 1¾ cups skim milk

salt and pepper

2 *is good* 4 medium tomatoes, sliced thinly

½ cup fresh bread crumbs *— optional*

¼ cup reduced-fat Cheddar cheese, grated

TO SERVE

whole-wheat bread

fresh salad

variation

You can stir 2 tablespoons of chopped fresh parsley into the pasta mixture in Step 3, if you like. Sprinkle the surface with parsley rather than scallions.

cook's tip

Cornstarch is usually mixed into a smooth paster ith a little liquid before . added to the remainin; liquid. This prevents the sauce turning lumpy.

1 Preheat the oven to 375°F/190°C. Bring a large pan of water to a boil and cook the pasta according to the instructions on the package. Drain well.

2 Meanwhile, heat the oil in a skillet and cook the mushrooms and all but a handful of the scallions for 4–5 minutes, until softened.

3 Place the cooked pasta in a bowl and mix in the scallions, mushrooms, tuna, and shrimp.

4 Blend the cornstarch with a little of the milk to make a paste. Pour the remaining milk into a pan and stir in the paste. Heat, stirring, until the sauce starts to thicken. Season well with salt and pepper. Add the sauce to the pasta mixture and mix well. Transfer to a large, ovenproof gratin dish and place on a baking sheet.

5 Arrange t slices over t' and sprinkle with the bread crumbs and cheese. Bake in the preheated oven for 25–30 minutes, or until golden. Serve sprinkled with the reserved scallions and accompanied with whole-wheat bread and salad.

indian cod with tomatoes

serves 4   **prep: 5 mins** ⟁   **cook: 25 mins** ⟁

Quick and easy—cod steaks are cooked in a rich tomato and coconut sauce to produce tender, succulent results.

INGREDIENTS

3 tbsp vegetable oil	1 tsp ground cumin
4 cod steaks, about 1-inch/2.5-cm thick	1 tsp ground turmeric
salt and pepper	½ tsp garam masala
1 onion, finely chopped	14 oz/400 g canned chopped tomatoes
2 garlic cloves, crushed	⅔ cup coconut milk
1 red bell pepper, seeded and chopped	1–2 tbsp chopped fresh cilantro
1 tsp ground coriander	or parsley

NUTRITIONAL INFORMATION

Calories	.194
Protein	.21g
Carbohydrate	.7g
Sugars	.6g
Fat	.9g
Saturates	.1g

variation

The mixture may be flavored with a tablespoonful of curry powder or curry paste instead of the mixture of spices in Step 2, if you wish.

cook's tip

The heat must be kept low in Step 2 to prevent the spices burning and losing their flavor. Frequent stirring will help to prevent them sticking to the bottom of the skillet.

1 Heat the oil in a skillet, add the fish steaks, season with salt and pepper and cook for 2–3 minutes, until browned on both sides but not cooked through. Remove from the pan and set aside.

2 Add the onion, garlic, red bell pepper, and spices and cook over very low heat for 2 minutes, stirring frequently. Add the tomatoes, bring to a boil and let simmer for 5 minutes.

3 Add the fish steaks to the skillet and let simmer gently for 8 minutes, or until the fish is cooked through. Remove from the skillet with a slotted spoon and keep warm on a serving dish.

4 Add the coconut milk and cilantro to the skillet and reheat gently. Spoon the sauce over the cod steaks and serve immediately.

catalan mussels

serves 4   **prep: 15 mins** ⏲   **cook: 15 mins** ♨

Mussels are cooked in a piquant tomato sauce with just a hint of spice. You can serve them hot, lukewarm in the Spanish style, or cold. Provide plenty of crusty bread or rolls to mop up the juices.

INGREDIENTS

4 lb 8 oz/2 kg live mussels, scrubbed
and debearded
5 tbsp olive oil
2 onions, chopped
2 garlic cloves, finely chopped
4 large tomatoes, peeled, seeded, and
finely chopped
1 bay leaf
1 tbsp brandy
½ tsp paprika
salt and pepper
crusty bread, to serve

NUTRITIONAL INFORMATION

Calories	.315
Protein	.28g
Carbohydrate	.11g
Sugars	.9g
Fat	.17g
Saturates	.3g

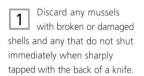

cook's tip

When buying mussels, choose ones that have a fresh, salty smell and undamaged shells. Do not pick any mussels that are heavy, as they may be full of sand, or any that feel very light, as they may be dead.

1 Discard any mussels with broken or damaged shells and any that do not shut immediately when sharply tapped with the back of a knife.

2 Heat the oil in a large, heavy-bottom pan or flameproof casserole. Add the onion and garlic and cook over low heat, stirring occasionally, for 5 minutes, or until softened. Add the tomatoes and bay leaf and cook, stirring occasionally, for an additional 5 minutes.

3 Stir in the brandy and paprika and season to taste with salt and pepper. Increase the heat, add the mussels, cover the pan and cook, shaking the pan occasionally, for 5 minutes, or until the shells have opened. Discard the bay leaf and any mussels that have not opened. Transfer the mussels to a warmed serving dish and pour the sauce over them. Serve immediately with crusty bread or let cool.

thai fragrant mussels

⏲ **cook: 5 mins**   ◔ **prep: 10 mins**   **serves 4**

*Lemon grass, galangal, and lime leaves delicately flavor and
perfume this simple and elegant dish. Serve with a chili sauce
for dipping, if you like.*

NUTRITIONAL INFORMATION	
Calories	133
Protein	26g
Carbohydrate	1g
Sugars	0g
Fat	3g
Saturates	1g

INGREDIENTS

4 lb 8 oz/2 kg live mussels, scrubbed
and debearded

2 lemon grass stalks, lightly crushed

2-inch/5-cm piece of galangal or
fresh gingerroot, bruised

5 kaffir lime leaves, shredded

3 garlic cloves

1¼ cups water

salt

cook's tip

Galangal is used extensively in
Southeast Asia. It is a member
of the ginger family, but is
spicier than fresh gingerroot.
It can be found in Asian food
stores. If it is unavailable, then
use fresh gingerroot instead.

1 Discard any mussels with broken or damaged shells and any that do not shut immediately when sharply tapped with the back of a knife.

2 Place the mussels, lemon grass, galangal, lime leaves, garlic, and water into a large, heavy-bottom pan or flameproof casserole and season to taste with salt. Bring to a boil, then cover and cook over high heat, shaking the pan occasionally, for 5 minutes, or until the shells have opened.

3 Remove and discard the flavorings and any mussels that have not opened. Divide the mussels between 4 soup bowls with a slotted spoon. Tilt the pan and let any sand settle, then spoon the cooking liquid over the mussels and serve immediately.

desserts

If the proof of the pudding is in the eating, then this is the chapter for you. While those great stand-bys, fresh fruit and pots of yogurt, certainly have a place in the busy cook's life, they can become tedious if served every night, and a homemade dessert makes a welcome change. Whether a family meal or a dinner party, dessert is the final, triumphant flourish and the great thing is that the range of hot and cold dishes which can be prepared at speed is surprisingly extensive. Bakes, fritters, creams, cheesecakes, and even light-as-air soufflés can be made in minutes and need no special skills or expertise.

There are tantalizing treats for the sweet-toothed, such as Almost Instant Toffee Pudding (see page 245) and Fried Bananas in Maple Syrup (see page 248); popular children's choices, such as Apple Fritters (see page 229) and Strawberry Baked Alaska (see page 241); and rich and creamy dishes for more sophisticated palates, such as Zabaglione (see page 234) and Lemon Posset (see page 242). Many of the recipes, while still taking only a short time in the kitchen, can be prepared in advance and so are ideal for entertaining. Cold desserts usually benefit from being chilled, even for just 30 minutes, but this doesn't have to cause delays. Because you can make them so quickly, do so before you begin to prepare the main course—they can then chill in the refrigerator while you are cooking and eating your meal.

sugar-topped fruit cake

serves 10 **prep: 15 mins** ⟳ **cook: 1 hr** ⟳

Soft apple purée and whole blackberries make this fruit cake delicious, and a sugar-cube topping adds crunch and sweetness.

INGREDIENTS

1 tbsp butter, for greasing

12 oz/350 g cooking apples

3 tbsp lemon juice

scant 2 cups whole-wheat self-rising flour

½ tsp baking powder

1 tsp ground cinnamon, plus extra for dusting

¾ cup prepared blackberries, thawed if frozen, plus extra to decorate

scant ⅞ cup firmly packed brown sugar

1 medium egg, beaten

scant 1 cup low fat mascarpone cheese

2 oz/55 g white or brown sugar cubes, lightly crushed

sliced eating apple, to decorate

NUTRITIONAL INFORMATION

Calories	227
Protein	. . . . .5g
Carbohydrate	. . . . .53g
Sugars	. . . . .30g
Fat	. . . . .1g
Saturates	. . . . .0.2g

variation

Try replacing the blackberries with blueberries. You can use the canned or frozen variety if fresh blueberries are not available.

cook's tip

Make sure that the apples are completely soft before beating them, to ensure a smooth texture in the finished cake.

1 Preheat the oven to 375°F/190°C. Grease a 2-lb/900-g loaf pan with the butter and line with parchment paper. Core, peel, and finely dice the apples. Place them in a pan with the lemon juice, bring to a boil, cover, and let simmer for 10 minutes until soft and pulpy. Beat well and let cool.

2 Sift the flour, baking powder, and cinnamon into a bowl, adding any husks that remain in the strainer. Stir in ½ cup of the blackberries and the sugar.

3 Make a well in the center of the ingredients and add the egg, mascarpone cheese, and cooled apple purée. Mix well

to incorporate thoroughly. Spoon the cake batter into the prepared loaf pan and smooth over the top.

4 Sprinkle with the remaining blackberries, pressing them down into the cake batter, and top with the crushed sugar cubes. Bake for 40–45 minutes. Let cool in the pan.

5 Remove the cake from the pan and peel away the lining paper. Serve dusted with cinnamon and decorated with extra blackberries and apple slices.

raspberry fusilli

serves 4   **prep: 5 mins** ◔   **cook: 20 mins** ♨

This is the ultimate in complete self-indulgence—a truly delicious dessert that tastes every bit as good as it looks.

INGREDIENTS

6 oz/175 g dried fusilli

1 lb 9 oz/700 g raspberries

2 tbsp superfine sugar

1 tbsp lemon juice

4 tbsp slivered almonds

3 tbsp raspberry liqueur

NUTRITIONAL INFORMATION

Calories 235

Protein 7g

Carbohydrate 36g

Sugars 20g

Fat 7g

Saturates 1g

variation

You could use any sweet berry for this dessert. Try strawberries or blackberries and use the correspondingly flavored fruit liqueur.

1 Bring a large pan of lightly salted water to a boil. Add the fusilli and cook for 8–10 minutes, or until tender but still firm to the bite. Drain the fusilli thoroughly, return to the pan, and let cool.

2 Using a spoon, firmly press 1 cup of the raspberries through a strainer

set over a mixing bowl to form a smooth purée. Place the purée in a small pan with the sugar and let simmer over low heat, stirring occasionally, for 5 minutes. Stir in the lemon juice and set the sauce aside until required.

3 Add the remaining raspberries to the fusilli in the pan and mix together

well. Transfer the raspberry and fusilli mixture to a serving dish.

4 Preheat the broiler to medium. Spread the almonds out on a cookie sheet and toast under the broiler for 1–2 minutes, until golden brown. Remove and let cool slightly.

5 Stir the raspberry liqueur into the reserved raspberry sauce and mix well until very smooth. Pour the sauce over the fusilli, sprinkle over the toasted almonds, and serve.

quick tiramisu

⏱ **cook: 0 mins**   ⏱ **prep: 15 mins**   **serves 4**

This quick version of one of the most widely-loved, traditional Italian desserts takes just minutes to make.

NUTRITIONAL INFORMATION	
Calories	.387
Protein	.9g
Carbohydrate	.22g
Sugars	.17g
Fat	.28g
Saturates	.15g

INGREDIENTS

1 cup mascarpone or
whole soft cheese

1 egg, separated

2 tbsp plain yogurt

2 tbsp superfine sugar

2 tbsp dark rum

2 tbsp strong black coffee

8 ladyfingers

2 tbsp grated semisweet chocolate

cook's tip

Mascarpone is an Italian soft cream cheese made from cow's milk. It has a rich, silky smooth texture and a deliciously creamy flavor. It can be eaten as it is with fresh fruits or flavored with coffee or chocolate.

1 Place the cheese in a large bowl, add the egg yolk and yogurt and beat until smooth.

2 Whisk the egg white until stiff but not dry, then whisk in the sugar and carefully fold into the cheese mixture. Divide half of the mixture between 4 sundae glasses.

3 Mix the rum and coffee together in a shallow dish. Dip the ladyfingers into the rum mixture, break them in half, or into smaller pieces if necessary, and divide between the glasses.

4 Stir any remaining coffee mixture into the remaining cheese mixture and divide between the glasses.

5 Sprinkle with the grated chocolate. Serve immediately, or let chill in the refrigerator until required.

carrot & ginger cake

serves 10 **prep: 15 mins** **cook: 1 hr 15 mins**

This melt-in-the-mouth version of a favorite cake has a fraction of the fat of the traditional cake, and is packed with vitamins.

INGREDIENTS

1 tbsp butter, for greasing	3 tbsp corn oil
1½ cups all-purpose flour	juice of 1 medium orange
1 tsp baking powder	
1 tsp baking soda	FROSTING
2 tsp ground ginger	1 cup low fat soft cheese
½ tsp salt	4 tbsp confectioners' sugar
scant ⅞ cup firmly packed brown sugar	1 tsp vanilla extract
8 oz/225 g carrots, grated	
2 pieces preserved ginger in syrup, drained and chopped	TO DECORATE
	grated carrot
1 oz/25 g fresh gingerroot, grated	preserved ginger
⅓ cup seedless raisins	ground ginger
2 medium eggs, beaten	

NUTRITIONAL INFORMATION

Calories	.249
Protein	.7g
Carbohydrate	.46g
Sugars	.28g
Fat	.6g
Saturates	.1g

variation

You could sprinkle the frosting with ground cinnamon instead of ground ginger if you prefer.

cook's tip

Using a loose-bottom cake pan will make it easier to turn out the cake, but be careful to line the pan well, with no gaps round the edges.

1 Preheat the oven to 350°F/180°C. Grease an 8-inch/20-cm round cake pan with the butter and line with parchment paper.

2 Sift the flour, baking powder, baking soda, ground ginger, and salt into a bowl. Stir in the sugar, carrots, preserved ginger, fresh gingerroot, and raisins. In a separate bowl, beat the eggs, oil and orange juice together, then pour into the cake batter. Mix together well.

3 Spoon the cake batter into the pan and bake in the oven for 1–1¼ hours, or until firm to the touch and the tip of a knife inserted into the center of the cake comes out clean.

4 To make the frosting, place the soft cheese in a large bowl and beat to soften. Sift in the confectioners' sugar and add the vanilla extract. Mix well.

5 Remove the cake from the pan and smooth the frosting over the top. Decorate the cake with grated carrot and ginger and serve.

tuscan puddings

serves 4　　　　**prep: 20 mins** ⏱　　　　**cook: 15 mins** ⏱

These mini baked ricotta puddings are delicious served warm or chilled and will keep in the refrigerator for 3–4 days.

INGREDIENTS

1 tbsp butter, for greasing

scant ½ cup mixed dry fruit

1⅛ cups ricotta cheese

3 egg yolks

¼ cup superfine sugar

1 tsp cinnamon

finely grated rind of 1 orange,

plus extra to decorate

crème fraîche or sour cream, to serve

(optional)

NUTRITIONAL INFORMATION

Calories	.293
Protein	.9g
Carbohydrate	.28g
Sugars	.28g
Fat	.17g
Saturates	.9g

cook's tip

Crème fraîche has a slightly sour, nutty taste and is very thick. It has the same fat content as heavy cream. It can be made by stirring cultured buttermilk into heavy cream and refrigerating overnight.

1 Preheat the oven to 350°F/180°C. Lightly grease 4 mini ovenproof bowls or ramekins with the butter.

2 Place the dry fruit in a bowl and cover with warm water. Let soak for 10 minutes.

3 Beat the ricotta cheese with the egg yolks in a bowl. Stir in the superfine sugar, cinnamon, and orange rind and mix to combine.

4 Drain the dry fruit in a strainer set over a bowl. Mix the drained fruit with the ricotta cheese mixture. Spoon the mixture into the bowls or ramekins and bake in the oven for 15 minutes. The tops of the puddings should be firm to the touch, but not brown.

5 Turn out the puddings and decorate them with grated orange rind. Serve warm or chilled with a spoonful of crème fraîche, if you like.

honey & nut nests

⏱ **cook: 1 hour**   ◔ **prep: 10 mins**   **serves 4**

Pistachios and honey are combined with crisp, cooked angel hair pasta in this unusual and attractive dessert.

NUTRITIONAL INFORMATION

Calories 802

Protein 13g

Carbohydrate 85g

Sugars 53g

Fat 48g

Saturates 16g

INGREDIENTS

salt

8 oz/225 g angel hair pasta

4 oz/115 g butter

generous 1¼ cups shelled pistachios, chopped

½ cup sugar

⅓ cup honey

⅔ cup water

2 tsp lemon juice

strained plain yogurt, to serve

cook's tip

Angel hair pasta is also known as *capelli d'angelo*. It is long and very fine, and is usually sold in small bunches that already resemble nests.

1 Preheat the oven to 350°F/180°C. Bring a large pan of lightly salted water to a boil. Add the angel hair pasta and cook for 8–10 minutes, or until tender but still firm to the bite. Drain the pasta and return to the pan. Add the butter and toss to coat the pasta thoroughly. Let cool.

2 Arrange 4 small tart or poaching rings on a cookie sheet. Divide the angel hair pasta into 8 equal quantities and spoon 4 of them into the rings. Press down lightly. Top the pasta with half of the nuts, then add the remaining pasta. Bake the nests in a preheated oven for 45 minutes, or until golden brown.

3 Meanwhile, place the sugar, honey, and water in a pan and bring to a boil over low heat, stirring constantly, until the sugar has dissolved completely. Let simmer for 10 minutes, add the lemon juice and let simmer for an additional 5 minutes.

4 Using a spatula, carefully transfer the cooked angel hair nests to a serving dish. Pour over the honey syrup, sprinkle over the remaining nuts, and let cool completely before serving. Serve the strained plain yogurt separately.

banana & lime cake

serves 10   **prep: 35 mins**   **cook: 45 mins**

This substantial cake is ideal served with a mid-afternoon cup of tea. The mashed bananas help to keep the cake moist, and the lime frosting gives it extra zing and zest.

INGREDIENTS

1 tbsp butter, for greasing

scant 2 cups all-purpose flour

1 tsp salt

1½ tsp baking powder

scant ⅞ cup firmly packed brown sugar

1 tsp grated lime rind

1 medium egg, beaten

1 medium banana, mashed with 1 tbsp lime juice

⅔ cup low fat mascarpone cheese

⅔ cup golden raisins

TOPPING

1 cup confectioners' sugar

1–2 tsp lime juice

½ tsp finely grated lime rind

TO DECORATE

banana chips

finely grated lime rind

variation

Replace the lime rind and juice with orange and the golden raisins with chopped apricots, if you prefer.

cook's tip

Banana chips are dried slices of banana, and can be found in the baking section of supermarkets, or in health food stores.

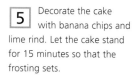

1 Preheat the oven to 350°F/180°C. Grease a deep 7-inch/18-cm round cake pan with the butter and line with parchment paper.

2 Sift the flour, salt, and baking powder into a mixing bowl and stir in the sugar and lime rind. Make a well in the center of the dry ingredients and add the egg, banana, mascarpone cheese, and golden raisins. Mix well until thoroughly incorporated.

3 Spoon the cake batter into the prepared pan and smooth the surface. Bake in the preheated oven for 40–45 minutes, until firm to the touch or until the tip of a knife inserted into the center comes out clean. Let cool for 10 minutes in the pan, then turn out onto a wire rack to cool completely.

4 To make the topping, sift the confectioners' sugar into a bowl and mix with the lime juice to form a soft, but not too runny, frosting. Stir in the lime rind. Drizzle the frosting over the cake, letting it run down the sides.

5 Decorate the cake with banana chips and lime rind. Let the cake stand for 15 minutes so that the frosting sets.

indian mango dessert

serves 4   **prep: 10 mins** (ᐸ   **cook: 0 mins** ⏲

Perhaps because the main course often tends to be spicy, Indian cooks will often serve a sweet, refreshing and creamy dessert as a contrast at the end of a meal.

INGREDIENTS

2 ripe mangoes
1¼ cups heavy cream, plus extra to decorate
2 tsp superfine sugar

NUTRITIONAL INFORMATION

Calories	.412
Protein	.2g
Carbohydrate	.15g
Sugars	.15g
Fat	.39g
Saturates	.24g

variation

Use other exotic fruits. Cut 14 oz/400 g guavas in half, sprinkle with lime juice and scoop out the flesh. Don't use kiwifruit as it curdles the cream.

1 Place a mango, on a cutting board, narrow-side down, and cut a thick slice lengthwise as close to the seed as possible. Turn the mango round and slice the other side as close to the seed as possible. Cut off any flesh remaining on the seed. Set aside a few unpeeled, thin mango slices for the decoration. Without cutting through the skin of the mango halves, score the flesh in the 2 thick slices in criss-cross lines about ½ inch/1 cm apart. Fold the halves inside out and slice off the cubes of flesh. Repeat with the second mango.

2 Place the mango flesh in a blender or food processor and process until a smooth purée forms.

3 Beat the cream with the sugar until stiff, then gently fold in the mango purée. Spoon into glass dishes, cover, and let chill in the refrigerator until required. Serve decorated with extra whipped cream and the reserved mango slices.

somerset pears

cook: 20 mins　　　　**prep: 5 mins**　　　　**serves 4**

The pears must be ripe but still quite firm for this dish. Choose a variety such as Anjou or Bartlett. Serve with vanilla ice cream or cream to create the perfect finale to a dinner party.

NUTRITIONAL INFORMATION	
Calories 139	
Protein 1g	
Carbohydrate 32g	
Sugars 32g	
Fat . . . . ,, 0g	
Saturates 0g	

INGREDIENTS

1 cup medium sweet cider

generous ¼ cup superfine sugar

thinly pared rind and juice of 1 lemon

pinch of freshly grated nutmeg

4 pears

variation

Pears are also delicious if they are poached gently in the same amount of red wine, superfine sugar, and a pinch of cloves.

1 Pour the cider into a large, heavy-bottom pan and add the sugar, lemon rind, lemon juice, and nutmeg. Heat gently, stirring constantly, until the sugar has dissolved.

2 Peel the pears using a swivel-blade vegetable peeler, but leave the stalks intact. Add them to the pan and poach gently, turning frequently, for 15 minutes.

3 Transfer the pears to warmed bowls with a slotted spoon. Increase the heat under the pan and stir the cooking liquid occasionally, until slightly reduced and syrupy. Spoon over the pears and serve immediately.

florentines

These luxury cookies will be popular at any time of the year, but make a particularly wonderful treat at Christmas.

INGREDIENTS

1³⁄₄ oz/50 g butter

¼ cup superfine sugar

1–2 tbsp all-purpose flour, sifted

generous ¼ cup almonds, chopped

scant ¼ cup chopped candied peel

2 tbsp raisins, chopped

2 tbsp candied cherries, chopped

finely grated rind of ¹⁄₂ lemon

4¹⁄₂ oz/125 g semisweet chocolate, melted

NUTRITIONAL INFORMATION

Calories 186

Protein 2g

Carbohydrate 22g

Sugars 19g

Fat 11g

Saturates 5g

variation

Replace the semisweet chocolate with white chocolate or, for a dramatic effect, cover half of the florentines in dark chocolate and half in white.

cook's tip

To melt the chocolate, break into even-size pieces and place in a heatproof bowl set over a pan of gently simmering water and stir until smooth.

1 Preheat the oven to 350°F/180°C. Line 2 large cookie sheets with parchment paper.

2 Heat the butter and superfine sugar in a small pan until the butter has just melted and the sugar has dissolved. Remove the pan from the heat.

3 Stir in the flour and mix well. Stir in the chopped almonds, candied peel, raisins, cherries, and lemon rind. Place teaspoonfuls of the cookie batter well apart on the prepared cookie sheets and bake in the preheated oven for 10 minutes, or until lightly golden.

4 As soon as the florentines are removed from the oven, press the edges into neat shapes while still on the cookie sheets, using a cookie cutter. Let cool on the cookie sheets until firm, then transfer to a wire rack to cool completely.

5 Spread the melted chocolate over the smooth side of each florentine. As the chocolate starts to set, mark wavy lines in it with a fork. Let the florentines stand until set, chocolate-side up.

charcooked pineapple

serves 4   prep: 10 mins   cook: 10 mins

Fresh pineapple slices are brushed with a buttery fresh ginger and brown sugar baste and cooked on the barbecue.

INGREDIENTS

1 fresh pineapple

GINGER BUTTER
4½ oz/125 g butter
generous ⅜ cup light brown sugar
1 tsp finely grated fresh gingerroot

TOPPING
1 cup mascarpone cheese
½ tsp ground cinnamon
1 tbsp light brown sugar

NUTRITIONAL INFORMATION	
Calories	.461
Protein	.5g
Carbohydrate	.45g
Sugars	.44g
Fat	.30g
Saturates	.20g

variation

If you prefer, substitute ½ teaspoon ground ginger for the fresh ginger. Light brown sugar gives the best flavor, but you can also use soft brown sugar.

1 Prepare the fresh pineapple by cutting off the spiky top. Peel the pineapple with a sharp knife, remove the "eyes," and cut the flesh into thick slices.

2 To make the ginger butter, place the butter, sugar, and ginger into a small pan and heat gently until melted. Transfer to a heatproof bowl and keep warm at the side of the barbecue, ready for basting the fruit.

3 To make the topping, mix the mascarpone cheese, cinnamon, and sugar together in a bowl. Cover and let chill in the refrigerator until ready to serve.

4 Brush the pineapple slices well with the ginger butter baste, then barbecue for 2 minutes on each side.

5 Serve the charcooked pineapple with a little extra ginger butter poured over. Top with a spoonful of the spiced mascarpone cheese.

italian chocolate truffles

cook: 5 mins   **prep: 5 mins**   **makes 24**

*These truffles, flavored with almonds and chocolate, are simplicity
itself to make. Served with coffee, they are the perfect end to a meal.*

NUTRITIONAL INFORMATION	
Calories	.82
Protein	.1g
Carbohydrate	.8g
Sugars	.7g
Fat	.5g
Saturates	.3g

INGREDIENTS

6 oz/175 g semisweet chocolate

2 tbsp almond-flavored or
orange-flavored liqueur

1½ oz/40 g unsalted butter

generous ⅜ cup confectioners' sugar

½ cup ground almonds

1¾ oz/50 g grated milk chocolate

variation

If you prefer, you can roll
the truffles in grated white
chocolate to give them a
constrasting coating.

1 Melt the semisweet
chocolate with the
liqueur in a heatproof bowl set
over a pan of simmering water,
stirring until well combined.

2 Add the butter and stir
until it has melted. Stir
in the confectioners' sugar and
the ground almonds. Let the
mixture stand in a cool place
until firm. Roll into 24 balls.

3 Place the grated
chocolate on a plate
and roll the truffles in the
chocolate to coat them.
Place the truffles in paper
candy cases and let chill in the
refrigerator until required.

apple fritters

cook: 8–10 mins

prep: 10 mins

serves 4

variation

Replace the apple with 1 small pineapple, peeled and cut into rings. Banana fritters would also be delicious. Use 4 bananas instead of apples.

Succulent apple rings, enclosed in crispy batter, and sprinkled with cinnamon sugar, are sure to become firm family favorites.

INGREDIENTS

corn oil, for deep-frying

1 large egg

pinch of salt

¾ cup water

⅜ cup all-purpose flour

2 tsp ground cinnamon

generous ¼ cup superfine sugar

4 eating apples, peeled and cored

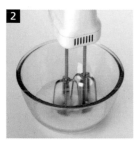

cook's tip

The best and easiest way to core an apple is to use an apple corer. Push the corer into the stalk end of the apple and twist to cut round the core, then pull it out and discard.

1 Pour the corn oil into a deep fryer or large, heavy-bottom pan and heat to 350–375°F/180–190°C, or until a cube of bread browns in 30 seconds.

2 Meanwhile, using an electric mixer, beat the egg and salt together until frothy, then quickly whisk in the water and flour. Do not overbeat the batter—it doesn't matter if it isn't completely smooth.

3 Mix the cinnamon and sugar together in a shallow dish and set aside.

4 Slice the apples into ¼-inch/5-mm thick rings. Spear with a fork, 1 slice at a time, and dip in the batter to coat. Add to the hot oil, in batches, and cook for 1 minute on each side, or until golden and puffed up. Remove with a slotted spoon and drain on paper towels. Keep warm while you cook the remaining batches. Transfer to a large serving plate, sprinkle with the cinnamon sugar, and serve.

vanilla ice cream

serves 6　　　　　**prep: 5 mins** ⏳　　　　　**cook: 15 mins** ⏳

This homemade version of real vanilla ice cream is absolutely delicious and so easy to make. A tutti-frutti variation is also provided.

INGREDIENTS

2½ cups heavy cream

1 vanilla bean

pared rind of 1 lemon

4 eggs, beaten, and 2 egg yolks

scant ⅞ cup superfine sugar

NUTRITIONAL INFORMATION

Calories	.626
Protein	.7g
Carbohydrate	.33g
Sugars	.33g
Fat	.53g
Saturates	.31g

variation

For tutti-frutti ice cream, follow the same method, omitting the vanilla bean, and stir in ½ cup mixed dry fruit soaked in sherry just before freezing.

1 Place the cream in a heavy-bottom pan over low heat and warm gently, whisking. Add the vanilla bean, lemon rind, eggs, and egg yolks to the pan, increase the heat and stir until the mixture reaches just below boiling point.

2 Reduce the heat to low and cook for 8–10 minutes, whisking the mixture, until thickened. Stir in the sugar, then let cool.

3 Strain the mixture through a strainer. Slit open the vanilla bean, scoop out the tiny black seeds and stir them into the cream.

4 Pour the mixture into a shallow freezer container with a lid and freeze overnight, until set. Scoop out to serve.

peaches & mascarpone

⏲ **cook: 10 mins**   ◔ **prep: 10 mins**   **serves 4**

*If you prepare these in advance, all you have to do is pop the
peaches on the barbecue when you are ready to serve them.*

NUTRITIONAL INFORMATION

Calories 301

Protein 6g

Carbohydrate 24g

Sugars 24g

Fat 20g

Saturates 9g

INGREDIENTS

4 peaches

¾ cup mascarpone cheese

⅜ cup pecans or walnuts, chopped

1 tsp corn oil

4 tbsp maple syrup

variation

You can use nectarines
instead of peaches for
this recipe. Remember to
choose ripe but firm fruit,
which will keep its shape
when barbecued.

1 Cut the peaches in half
and remove the pits.
If you are preparing this recipe
in advance, press the peach
halves together again and
wrap in plastic wrap
until required.

2 Mix the mascarpone
cheese and nuts
together in a bowl until well
combined. Let chill in the
refrigerator until required.

3 To serve, brush the
peaches with a little oil
and place on a rack set over
medium hot coals. Barbecue
for 5–10 minutes, turning
once, until hot.

4 Transfer the peaches to
a serving dish and top
with the mascarpone mixture.
Drizzle the maple syrup over
the top and serve at once.

pineapple bake

serves 6   **prep: 15 mins**   **cook: 10 mins**

A deliciously tropical taste of warm, fresh pineapple and a light-as-air rum-flavored topping will bring a smile to everyone's face.

INGREDIENTS

1 pineapple	1 egg yolk
4 tbsp golden raisins	1 tbsp cornstarch
2 tbsp raisins	½ tsp vanilla extract
4 tbsp maple syrup	¼ tsp ground ginger
4 tbsp white rum, such as Bacardi	2 egg whites
	2 tbsp brown sugar

NUTRITIONAL INFORMATION

Calories 240

Protein 3g

Carbohydrate 53g

Sugars 47g

Fat 1g

Saturates 0g

variation

For a slightly crunchier topping, replace the brown sugar with the same amount of raw brown sugar,

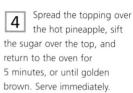

cook's tip

There are two important points to note: make sure that you buy genuine maple syrup (not maple-flavored syrup) and pure vanilla extract (rather than artificial, which is made from clove oil).

1 Preheat the oven to 475°F/240°C. Using a sharp knife, cut off the leafy pineapple top and a 1-inch/2.5-cm slice from the base and discard. Stand the pineapple upright on a large cutting board and slice off the skin in strips. Use the tip of the knife to remove any "eyes" and slice the pineapple in half lengthwise. Cut out the core,

then slice each pineapple half horizontally into slices.

2 Arrange the pineapple slices in a large ovenproof dish and sprinkle the golden raisins and raisins over them. Drizzle with half the maple syrup and half the rum. Bake in the preheated oven for 5 minutes.

3 Meanwhile, mix the remaining maple syrup and rum, egg yolk, cornstarch, vanilla, and ginger together in a bowl. Whisk the egg whites in a separate, spotlessly clean, greasefree bowl until soft peaks form. Stir 2 tablespoons of the egg whites into the egg yolk mixture, then fold all the egg yolk mixture into the whites.

4 Spread the topping over the hot pineapple, sift the sugar over the top, and return to the oven for 5 minutes, or until golden brown. Serve immediately.

zabaglione

serves 6   **prep: 5 mins** ⏲   **cook: 5 mins** ⏲

This rich, creamy, Italian dessert must be served as soon as it is ready, but fortunately it takes only moments to prepare.

INGREDIENTS

4 egg yolks

generous ⅓ cup superfine sugar

½ cup Marsala wine

NUTRITIONAL INFORMATION

Calories	115
Protein	2g
Carbohydrate	14g
Sugars	14g
Fat	4g
Saturates	1g

1 Using an electric mixer, beat the egg yolks with the sugar in a heatproof bowl until pale and creamy.

2 Set the bowl over a pan of barely simmering water. Make sure that the base of the bowl does not touch the surface of the water, or the yolks will scramble. Gradually beat in the Marsala and continue beating until the zabaglione is thick, creamy, and has increased in volume.

3 Divide the zabaglione between 6 wine glasses and serve immediately.

variation

Marsala is the usual wine used in this classic dessert, but other wines and spirits can be used, such as sherry or rum. Serve with amaretti cookies, if you like.

broiled peaches & cream

cook: 4 mins   **prep: 10 mins**   **serves 4**

*Broiled fruit makes a great dessert, not just because it is quick
and easy, but also because it tastes and looks so delicious.*

NUTRITIONAL INFORMATION	
Calories 280	
Protein 4g	
Carbohydrate 35g	
Sugars 35g	
Fat 15g	
Saturates 9g	

INGREDIENTS

4 large peaches

2 tbsp brown sugar

½ tsp ground cinnamon

1¼ cups sour cream

4 tbsp superfine sugar

1 Preheat the broiler to medium. Blanch the peaches in boiling water for 1 minute. Refresh under cold running water, then peel, halve, pit, and slice. Arrange the slices in 4 individual flameproof dishes.

2 Mix the brown sugar and cinnamon together and sprinkle the mixture over the peaches. Spoon the sour cream on top, then sprinkle 1 tablespoon of superfine sugar over each dish.

3 Cook under the preheated broiler for 2–3 minutes, or until the superfine sugar has melted and caramelized. Serve immediately or let cool.

cook's tip

To pit peaches, cut vertically round the fruit, then twist each half in opposite directions to reveal the pit. Using the tip of a knife, prise the pit out, lift it out with your fingers and discard.

broiled fruit kabobs

🕘 cook: 10 mins

🕘 prep: 10 mins, plus
10 mins marinating

serves 4

NUTRITIONAL INFORMATION

Calories 176

Protein 2g

Carbohydrate 30g

Sugars 27g

Fat 6g

Saturates 1g

variation

You can use other types of fruit for these kabobs, such as seedless grapes, mango slices and papaya chunks.

Use your time economically. Mix the marinade, then drop the pieces of fruit into it as you prepare them. Preheat the broiler while the fruit is marinating in the luscious mixture of hazelnut oil, lime juice, and honey.

INGREDIENTS

2 tbsp hazelnut oil

2 tbsp honey

juice and finely grated rind of 1 lime

2 pineapple rings, halved

8 strawberries

1 pear, peeled, cored, and thickly sliced

1 banana, peeled and thickly sliced

2 kiwifruit, peeled and quartered

1 carambola, cut into 4 slices

cook's tip

Honeys vary widely in flavor and the best quality, with a distinctive taste, is usually made from a single type of blossom. For this recipe, try orange blossom, acacia, or lime flower.

1 Preheat the broiler to medium. Mix the hazelnut oil, honey, lime juice, and rind together in a large, shallow, nonmetallic dish. Add the fruit and turn to coat. Let marinate for 10 minutes.

2 Thread the fruit alternately onto 4 long metal skewers, starting with a piece of pineapple and ending with a slice of carambola.

3 Brush the kabobs with the marinade and cook under the preheated hot broiler, brushing frequently with the marinade, for 5 minutes. Turn the kabobs over, brush with the marinade again and broil for an additional 5 minutes. Serve immediately.

fruit packages

serves 4   **prep: 15 mins** ⟲   **cook: 10 mins** ⏱

Children in particular enjoy this fun way of serving food and you can use virtually any of their favorite fruits. Use orange juice for young diners and orange liqueur for adults.

INGREDIENTS

unsalted butter, for greasing	2 tbsp superfine sugar
2 apples	2 tbsp orange liqueur or orange juice
2 bananas	2 tbsp slivered almonds
2 oranges	

NUTRITIONAL INFORMATION

Calories	.206
Protein	.3g
Carbohydrate	.35g
Sugars	.34g
Fat	.6g
Saturates	.2g

variation

Use other fruits, including hulled strawberries, slices of melon, mango and papaya, mandarin segments, and pear chunks, if you prefer.

cook's tip

Be careful when opening up the packages after cooking as they will be extremely hot. It is best if the packages are left to cool slightly before serving.

1 Preheat the oven to 475°F/240°C. Cut 4 large squares of foil and lightly grease with butter. Quarter and core the apples (but do not peel), then slice. Peel and slice the bananas. Peel the oranges, taking care to remove all the pith, then cut into segments and discard the membranes.

2 Place all the fruit in a large bowl and sprinkle the sugar over it. Add the orange liqueur and sprinkle with the almonds. Mix well.

3 Divide the fruit between the pieces of foil and wrap securely into neat packages. Place the packages on a large baking sheet and bake in the preheated oven for 10 minutes. Transfer to serving plates, open up the packages slightly, and serve.

grape brûlée

serves 4   **prep: 5 mins, plus 6 hrs ⏲ chilling (optional)**   **cook: 8 mins ⏲**

Although this dessert takes hardly any time to prepare, with only a few minutes needed to caramelize the topping, it is best served chilled. For the ideal grape brûlée, make it at least six hours or up to two days in advance.

INGREDIENTS

1¼ cups seedless grapes, halved

1 cup heavy cream

2 tbsp brandy

4 tsp superfine sugar

4 tbsp raw brown sugar

NUTRITIONAL INFORMATION	
Calories 379	
Protein 1g	
Carbohydrate 31g	
Sugars 31g	
Fat 27g	
Saturates 17g	

variation

For a lower-fat version, replace the heavy cream with plain yogurt and use either red or green grapes.

1 Set aside about 16 of the grape halves for decoration and place the rest in a shallow, flameproof dish.

2 Lightly whip the cream, then beat in the brandy and superfine sugar. Spread the cream over the grapes. If there is time, let chill in the refrigerator (with the reserved grapes) for at least 6 hours.

3 To serve, preheat the broiler to medium. Sprinkle the raw brown sugar evenly over the cream and place under the preheated broiler for about 8 minutes, or until bubbling and caramelized. Decorate with the reserved grape halves and serve.

strawberry baked alaska

⏱ **cook: 3–5 mins**   ◔ **prep: 10 mins**   **serves 6**

A first choice for children, and even adults will admit to enjoying the contrast between the cold ice cream and the warm meringue in this perennial favorite. You can use a homemade or store-bought sponge cake for the base.

NUTRITIONAL INFORMATION

Calories	.464
Protein	.9g
Carbohydrate	.63g
Sugars	.51g
Fat	.21g
Saturates	.9g

INGREDIENTS

9-inch/23-cm round sponge cake

2 tbsp sweet sherry or orange juice

5 egg whites

scant ¾ cup superfine sugar

2½ cups strawberry ice cream

generous 1 cup fresh strawberries, halved, plus whole strawberries, to serve

cook's tip

For the perfect meringue, bring the egg whites to room temperature before whisking. It is worth noting that the fresher the eggs, the greater the volume of the meringue.

1 Preheat the oven to 475°F/240°C. Place the sponge cake in a large, shallow, ovenproof dish and sprinkle with the sherry or orange juice.

2 Whisk the egg whites in a spotlessly clean, greasefree bowl until stiff. Continue to whisk, gradually adding the sugar, until very stiff and glossy.

3 Working quickly, cover the top of the cake with the ice cream and then top with the strawberry halves. Spread the meringue over the cake, making sure that the ice cream is completely covered. Bake in the preheated oven for 3–5 minutes, or until the meringue is golden brown. Serve immediately, with whole strawberries.

lemon posset

serves 4　　　　**prep: 10 mins** ⏲　　　　**cook: 0 mins** ⏱

This is a hugely rich and self-indulgent dessert, but the sharpness of the lemon gives it a wonderfully refreshing flavor.

INGREDIENTS

grated rind and juice of 1 large lemon

4 tbsp dry white wine

generous ¼ cup superfine sugar

1¼ cups heavy cream

2 egg whites

lemon slices, to decorate

cats' tongues, to serve

variation

Replace the lemon with the grated rind and juice of 1 orange, decorate with orange slices, and serve with amaretti cookies, if you prefer.

1 Mix the lemon rind, lemon juice, wine, and sugar together in a bowl. Stir until the sugar has dissolved. Add the cream and beat with an electric mixer until soft peaks form.

2 Whisk the egg whites in a separate, spotlessly clean, greasefree bowl until stiff, then carefully fold them into the cream mixture.

3 Spoon the mixture into tall glasses and let chill in the refrigerator until required. Serve decorated with lemon slices and accompanied by the cats' tongues.

cook's tip

Use only the very freshest eggs for this dish. It is not advisable to serve any dishes containing raw eggs to the very young or old, the infirm, or anyone whose immune system has been compromised.

almost instant toffee pudding

⏲ **cook: 15 mins**   ⏱ **prep: 10 mins**   **serves 6**

This is the ideal dessert for a midweek family supper in the fall or winter, when you have had a busy day and cold weather has sharpened everyone's appetite.

INGREDIENTS

2 eggs	4 oz/115 g unsalted butter
generous ⅓ cup milk	1 tbsp corn oil
pinch of ground cinnamon	generous ¼ cup brown sugar
6 slices of white bread, crusts removed	4 tbsp golden syrup

variation

Instead of the bread triangles, cut the bread into different shapes, such as fingers or small squares.

cook's tip

Keep the cooked bread warm in a medium–hot oven while making the toffee sauce. For a touch of indulgence, serve with some whipped cream.

1 Using a fork, beat the eggs with 6 tablespoons of the milk and the cinnamon in a large, shallow dish. Cut the bread into triangles and place in the dish, in batches if necessary, to soak for 2–3 minutes.

2 Melt half the butter with half the oil in a heavy-bottom skillet. Add the bread triangles, in batches, and cook for 2 minutes on each side, or until golden brown, adding a little more butter and oil as necessary Remove with a spatula, drain on paper towels, transfer to serving plates, and keep warm.

3 Add the remaining butter and milk to the skillet with the sugar and golden syrup and cook, stirring constantly, until hot and bubbling. Pour the toffee sauce over the bread triangles and serve.

speedy apricot cheesecake

serves 6

prep: 15 mins, plus 🕑
40 mins chilling

cook: 2–3 mins 🕑

This delicately flavored cheesecake needs no baking and is based on pantry ingredients, although you will need to buy cottage cheese and cream.

INGREDIENTS

15 oz/425 g canned apricot halves
in syrup

1½ cups cottage cheese

generous ⅜ cup superfine sugar

grated rind and juice of 1 lemon

1 tbsp gelatin powder

⅔ cup heavy cream

BASE

2 oz/55 g unsalted butter, plus extra
for greasing

4 oz/115 g graham crackers, crushed

½ tsp ground cinnamon

TO DECORATE

canned apricots, cut into slices

slivered almonds

NUTRITIONAL INFORMATION

Calories 437

Protein 12g

Carbohydrate 42g

Sugars 31g

Fat 26g

Saturates 16g

variation

Replace the canned apricot halves with other canned fruit, such as peaches, plums, or pitted cherries. Alternatively, use fresh fruit, such as strawberries.

cook's tip

Crush the graham crackers for the base in a food processor or place them in a large plastic bag and crush with a rolling pin until crumbs form.

1 Grease a 7-inch/18-cm loose-bottom, round cake pan with butter. To make the base, heat the butter gently in a small pan until just melted. Remove from the heat and stir in the graham cracker crumbs and cinnamon. Spoon the mixture into the pan and press it evenly over the base. Let chill in the refrigerator while you make the filling.

2 Drain the apricots and set aside the syrup. Place the apricots in a food processor and process until a smooth purée forms. Scrape the purée into a bowl. Rub the cottage cheese through a strainer into the bowl and beat in the sugar, lemon rind, and lemon juice until smooth.

3 Place 2 tablespoons of the reserved syrup in a small heatproof bowl and sprinkle the gelatin on the surface. Let stand for a few minutes to soften. Set the bowl over a pan of barely simmering water and stir until the gelatin has completely dissolved. Let cool while you whip the cream until thick. Stir the gelatin syrup into the

apricot mixture, then fold in the cream. Spread the filling over the base and let chill in the refrigerator until set. Decorate the top with apricot slices and almonds before serving.

fried bananas in maple syrup

serves 4   **prep: 5 mins** ⟳   **cook: 4 mins** ⟳

This almost instant dessert looks good and tastes delicious. For an extra treat, serve it with vanilla ice cream or plain yogurt.

INGREDIENTS

3 tbsp unsalted butter

6 bananas, peeled and diagonally sliced

6 tbsp maple syrup

4 tbsp slivered almonds, to decorate

NUTRITIONAL INFORMATION	
Calories 376	
Protein 4g	
Carbohydrate 61g	
Sugars 55g	
Fat 14g	
Saturates 6g	

1 Melt the butter in a large, heavy-bottom skillet. Add the bananas and cook over low heat for 45 seconds on each side.

2 Add the syrup and cook for an additional 2 minutes, or until the banana slices have softened.

3 Transfer the bananas to warmed serving dishes, sprinkle with slivered almonds, and serve immediately.

variation

Substitute the bananas with other fruit, such as pineapple rings or apple slices, if you like.

veiled country lass

⏲ **cook: 5 mins**   ⏲ **prep: 10 mins, plus**   **serves 6**
                                 30 mins chilling (optional)

This is a traditional Danish dessert made in layers, so it looks
especially attractive in a glass serving dish.

NUTRITIONAL INFORMATION	
Calories 539	
Protein 4g	
Carbohydrate 72g	
Sugars 57g	
Fat 28g	
Saturates 17g	

INGREDIENTS

8 oz/225 g rye bread, crusts removed

2 tbsp superfine sugar

2 tbsp unsalted butter

2 lb/900 g apple purée or applesauce

⅔ cup black currant jelly

1¼ cups heavy cream

cook's tip

The contrasts in this dessert
derive from using rye bread for
the crumbs, which has a
distinctive flavor and texture.
You could use German black
bread, made from a mixture of
rye and cornmeal.

1 Tear the bread into
pieces, place in a food
processor and process until
crumbs form. Transfer to a
bowl and stir in the sugar.

2 Melt the butter
in a large, heavy-
bottom skillet, add the bread
crumb mixture and cook
over medium heat, stirring
occasionally, for 3–5 minutes,

or until crisp. Remove the
skillet from the heat and let
cool slightly.

3 Spoon half the apple
purée into the base
of a glass serving dish. Cover
the purée with half the jelly,
then spoon on half the bread
crumb mixture. Repeat these
layers, ending with the bread
crumb mixture.

4 Using an electric mixer,
beat the cream until
thickened and stiff, then
spread it over the top of the
dessert. If you have time, let
chill for 30 minutes in the
refrigerator before serving.

lemon soufflé

🕒 **cook: 25 mins**   🕐 **prep: 5 mins**   **serves 6**

NUTRITIONAL INFORMATION	
Calories	177
Protein	. . . . .7g
Carbohydrate	. . . . .15g
Sugars	. . . . .12g
Fat	. . . . .10g
Saturates	. . . . .5g

A hot soufflé makes a spectacular end to a meal and this delicious, lemon-flavored dessert is the perfect palate cleanser. All hot soufflés will collapse disappointingly if left to stand, so make sure that you serve it as soon as it is ready.

INGREDIENTS

2 tbsp unsalted butter, plus extra for greasing

¼ cup confectioners' sugar

1¼ cups milk

scant ¼ cup all-purpose flour

grated rind and juice of 1 lemon

5 egg yolks

2 tbsp superfine sugar

6 egg whites

variation

Use the grated rind and juice of 1 orange instead of the lemon, if you prefer.

cook's tip

If you are planning to serve this delicious dessert to guests at a dinner party, you can prepare the soufflé up to the end of Step 2 in advance.

1 Preheat the oven to 350°F/180°C. Grease a 6-cup soufflé dish with butter and dust the bottom and sides with confectioners' sugar. Pour the milk into a small, heavy-bottom pan and bring to simmering point.

2 Meanwhile, melt the butter in a separate heavy-bottom pan over low heat. Remove from the heat and stir in the flour until a smooth paste forms. Gradually stir in the hot milk. Return to the heat and cook, stirring, for 2 minutes, or until thickened and smooth. Stir in the lemon rind and juice and set aside.

3 Beat the egg yolks with the superfine sugar until pale, then gradually stir them into the lemon mixture, adding only a little at a time.

4 Whisk the egg whites in a spotlessly clean, greasefree bowl until stiff peaks form. Fold the egg whites into the lemon mixture. Spoon into the dish and bake in the preheated oven for 20 minutes, or until risen and golden brown. Serve.

chocolate fondue

serves 6 **prep: 10 mins** ⏲ **cook: 5 mins** ♨

What could be quicker and easier than letting your guests serve themselves? This treat for those with a sweet tooth is traditionally served after a day on the ski slopes.

INGREDIENTS

selection of fresh fruit, such as apples, bananas, pears, seedless grapes, peaches, and oranges

juice of 1 lemon (optional)

small sponge or Madeira cake

8 oz/225 g semisweet chocolate, broken into pieces

6 tbsp heavy cream

2 tbsp dark rum

½ cup confectioners' sugar

NUTRITIONAL INFORMATION	
Calories	.698
Protein	.7g
Carbohydrate	.83g
Sugars	.70g
Fat	.39g
Saturates	.19g

variation

Use white chocolate instead of the semisweet chocolate and use other types of fruit, such as strawberries, grapes, or pineapple chunks.

cook's tip

Make sure that the chocolate is melted over very low heat. If the chocolate is too hot, then it may burn and turn grainy. Do not let any water splash on to the chocolate, otherwise it will seize and is unusuable.

1 Prepare the fruit according to type, cutting it into bite-size pieces. Brush apples, pears, and bananas with a little lemon juice to prevent them discoloring. Cut the sponge cake into cubes. Arrange the fruit and cake on several serving plates.

2 Place the chocolate and cream in the top of a double boiler and heat gently, stirring constantly, until melted and smooth. Alternatively, melt the chocolate and cream in a heatproof bowl set over a pan of barely simmering water. Remove the pan or bowl from the heat.

3 Stir in the rum and sugar. Pour the mixture into a ceramic fondue pot set over a burner and hand the fruit and cake separately. Each guest can then spear their chosen piece and dip it in the hot chocolate mixture.

A

anchovy sauce 194
angler fish in ruby grapefruit sauce 179
antipasto volente 66
apple fritters 229
apricot cheesecake 246
artichoke soup 22

B

bacon with corn salad 63
baked fennel 95
balti shrimp 203
banana & lime cake 220
basic recipes 13
bean & vegetable soup 20
beef
    kabobs 123
    & potato soup 35
    satay 64
    spaghetti & meatballs 146
    steak in orange sauce 126
    stock 13
    stroganoff 122
    tournedos Rossini 125
bell pepper salad 48
black butter sauce 185
blackened fish 174
broiled scallops & prawns with citrus
    butter 191
bruschetta 62
butterflied squab chickens 168

C

Caesar salad 85
Calabrian mushroom soup 18
Caribbean cook-up rice 103
carrots
    & dal soup 40
    & ginger cake 216
    & orange soup 27
Catalan mussels 208
charcooked pineapple 226
check list 12
cheese
    aigrettes 109
    fritters 108
    haddock in a jacket 173
    old English soup 26
    sauce 137
    tagliarini with gorgonzola 51
chef's salad 86
chicken

braised in red wine 163
butterflied squab chickens 168
cacciatore 167
Chinese 158
cordon bleu 156
garlic & herb 166
goujons 97
with green olives 164
honey-glazed 160
& leek soup 38
satay 64
sesame ginger 76
stock 13
tarragon 161
teriyaki 157
Chinese dishes
    chicken 158
    omelet 56
chocolate fondue 252
chunky potato & beef soup 35
citrus butter 191
cod
    Mediterranean 184
    with tomatoes 206
corn
    Indonesian balls 118
    spicy fritters 58
crab
    Creole 197
    partan bree 39
    soup 33
    Thai golden pouches 61
cream of pea soup 24
creamy mushroom sauce 135
crispy seaweed 57
cured meats with olives & tomatoes 72

D

dal & carrot soup 40
deep-fried seafood 98
dipping platter 99
dressings
    Thousand Island 13
    Vinaigrette 13

E

eggs
    Benedict 114
    Chinese omelet 56
    exotic mushroom omelets 112
    omelets with fines herbes 113
    zuppa pavese 31

eggplant dipping platter 99
equipment 10–11
exotic mushroom omelets 112

F

fajitas 71
fast-food techniques 7
fillets of red snapper & pasta 198
Finnan haddie 177
fish
    angler fish in ruby grapefruit sauce 179
    antipasto volente 66
    balti shrimp 203
    blackened 174
    canned 8
    Catalan mussels 208
    crab Creole 197
    deep-fried seafood 98
    fillets of red snapper & pasta 198
    Finnan haddie 177
    gamberi fritti 196
    haddock in a cheese jacket 173
    Indian cod with tomatoes 206
    lobster thermidor 193
    Mediterranean cod 184
    noodles with chile & shrimp 188
    pan-fried scallops & shrimps 46
    & potato pâté 92
    salmon with watercress cream 180
    scallops on horseback 46
    scallops on skewers 190
    sesame shrimp toasts 54
    shrimp pasta bake 204
    shrimp in anchovy sauce 194
    skate in black butter sauce 185
    smoked trout with pears 53
    sole meunière 183
    spicy crab soup 33
    Thai fragrant mussels 209
    Thai shrimp curry 202
    trout with almonds 176
    trout with smoked bacon 200
    Veracruz red snapper 186
flambéed shrimp 50
florentines 224
forward planning 10–11
fresh spaghetti & meatballs 146
fried dishes
    bananas in maple syrup 248
    green tomatoes 117
fritters
    apple 229

index

apple 229
  cheese 108
  peanut 119
  spicy corn 58
fruit packages 238

G

gamberi fritti 196
gammon in Madeira sauce 136
garlic
  croûtons 85
  & herb chicken 166
grape brûlée 240
Greek salad 87
grilled dishes 7
  fruit kabobs 237
  peaches & cream 235
guacamole 69

H

haddock
  in a cheese jacket 173
  Finnan 177
ham & asparagus rolls 137
honey & nut nests 219
honey-glazed chicken 160
hummus 68

I

Indian dishes
  cod with tomatoes 206
  mango dessert 222
Indonesian corn balls 118
Italian chocolate truffles 227

K

kabobs
  beef 123
  broiled scallops & shrimp 191
  grilled fruit 237
  scallops on skewers 190

L

lamb
  with bay & lemon 141
  with olives 140
  & rice soup 34
  Spanish cutlets 138
  stir-fried 143
leek & chicken soup 38
lemon
  posset 242

soufflé 251
lentil pâté 90
lobster thermidor 193

M

Madeira sauce 136
mascarpone & spinach soup 23
Mediterranean cod 184
menu-planning 10
Mexican tomato salad 82
mozzarella & tomatoes 75
mushrooms
  Calabrian soup 18
  & noodle soup 36
  sauce 135
  soup 30
mussels
  Catalan 208
  Thai fragrant 209

N

Neapolitan dishes
  pork steaks 130
  veal cutlets 148
noodles 9
  with chile & shrimp 188
  & mushroom soup 36
  Singapore 107

O

old English cheese soup 26
omelets
  Chinese 56
  exotic mushroom 112
  with fines herbes 113
onions
  gravy 144
  soup 44
orange sauce 126, 155

P

pan-fried scallops & shrimp 47
pantry tuna 111
partan bree 39
pasta 9
  fillets of red snapper 198
  fresh spaghetti & meatballs 146
  shrimp bake 204
  spaghetti alla carbonara 100
  tagliarini with gorgonzola 51
  & tomato soup 19
pâtés

lentil 90
  smoked fish & potato 92
pea soup 24
peaches & mascarpone 231
peanut fritters 119
pineapple bake 232
pork
  in creamy mushroom sauce 135
  with fennel & juniper 131
  Neapolitan steaks 130
  Singapore noodles 107
  stir-fry 132
  Thai golden pouches 61
  toad in the hole 144
  Virginian chops 129
potatoes 9
  & beef soup 35
  cheese fritters 108
  Russian salad 88
  & smoked fish pâté 92
  veal Italienne 150
prosciutto & figs 74
pumpkin soup 16

R

raspberry fusilli 214
red lentil soup with yogurt 42
red mullet & pasta 198
rice
  Caribbean cook-up 103
  & lamb soup 34
  speedy vegetable pilau 104
ruby grapefruit sauce 179
Russian salad 88

S

salade Niçoise 81
salads 7
  bell pepper 48
  Caesar 85
  chef's 86
  dressings 12
  Greek 87
  Mexican tomato 82
  Russian 88
salmon with watercress cream 180
sauces
  anchovy 194
  black butter 185
  cheese 137
  creamy mushroom 135
  Hollandaise 114

onion gravy 144
orange 126, 155
ready-made 8
ruby grapefruit 179
watercress cream 180
scallops
    on horseback 46
    pan-fried 47
    & shrimp with citrus butter 191
    on skewers 190
sesame
    ginger chicken 76
    shrimp toasts 54
shallots à la Grecque 94
shrimp
    in anchovy sauce 194
    antipasto volente 66
    balti 203
    broiled 191
    flambéed 50
    gamberi fritti 196
    noodles with chile 188
    pan-fried 47
    pasta bake 204
    sesame toasts 54
    Singapore noodles 107
    Thai curry 202
Singapore noodles 107
skate in black butter sauce 185
smoked fish
    & potato pâté 92
    trout with pears 53
sole meunière 183
Somerset pears 223
soups
    artichoke 22
    Calabrian mushroom 18
    carrot & orange 27
    chicken & leek 38
    chunky potato & beef 35
    cream of pea 24
    lamb & rice 34
    mushroom 30
    mushroom & noodle 36
    old English cheese 26
    partan bree 39
    pumpkin 16
    red lentil with yogurt 42
    spicy crab 33
    spicy dal & carrot 40
    spinach & mascarpone 23
    thick onion 44

tomato 28
tomato & pasta 19
vegetable & bean 20
yogurt & spinach 43
zuppa pavese 31
spaghetti
    alla carbonara 100
    & meatballs 146
Spanish cutlets 138
speedy vegetable pilau 104
spicy dishes
    corn fritters 58
    crab soup 33
    dal & carrot soup 40
spinach
    & mascarpone soup 23
    & yogurt soup 43
steak in orange sauce 126
stir-fries 7
    chicken teriyaki 157
    lamb 143
    pork 132
stock 13
stores 6, 7–8, 10
strawberry baked Alaska 241
stuffed tomatoes 116
sugar-topped fruit cake 212

T
tagliarini with gorgonzola 51
tarragon chicken 161
Thai dishes
    fragrant mussels 209
    golden pouches 61
    shrimp curry 202
thick onion soup 44
Thousand Island Dressing 13
time-saving tips 7–9, 12
tiramisu 215
toad in the hole with onion gravy 144
toffee pudding 245
tomatoes
    fried green 117
    Mexican salad 82
    & mozzarella 75
    & pasta soup 19
    paste 8–9
    soup 28
    stuffed 116
tournedos Rossini 125
trout
    with almonds 176

with pears 53
with smoked bacon 200
tuna
    antipasto volente 66
    pantry 111
turkey breasts with orange sauce 155
Tuscan puddings 218

V
vanilla ice cream 230
veal
    Italienne 150
    Neapolitan cutlets 148
    in a rose petal sauce 152
vegetables 7
    & bean soup 20
    peelers 11
    ready-prepared 8
    speedy pilau 104
    stock 13
vegetarian fajitas 71
veiled country lass 249
Veracruz red snapper 186
vinaigrette 13
Virginian pork chops 129

W
Western dishes 6

Y
yogurt
    red lentil soup 42
    & spinach soup 43
York ham & asparagus rolls 137

Z
zabaglione 234
zuppa pavese 31